The Chaos of My Mind

a bipolar memoir

ELLEN NORTHCOTT

ELLEN NORTHCOTT

For Jason, who makes life worth living
and for
Meredith, without whom I wouldn't still be living it.

Contents

Author's Note

This memoir evolved from a manic novel, to a truthful story, to a suicide note and finally to a book. I have stuck to the facts as far as I remember them, using much of what I had written as I was experiencing it. However, by necessity, this book is influenced by my bias at the time events occurred, and the ability of my memory to recreate scenes from the past. Some names and details have been changed to protect the anonymity of those involved.

Prologue

"Mostly I would like to say thank you to Jason for your love. You are my best friend, my support and the keeper of my sanity."

I locked eyes with Jason. His smart black tuxedo and styled hair was so different from his normal scruffy appearance, but the love shining out of his eyes was the same. I felt so incredibly lucky to be marrying this man. After six years I was still falling slightly deeper in love with him everyday. As I finished my speech my brother extracted the single red rose from its hiding place and passed it to me.

"For your honesty, generosity, kindness, love, smiles and laughter; may this rose always remind you of falling in love." Jason stood up as I gave him the rose and the shouts of "Kiss, kiss!" exploded around the room.

As we sat down still holding hands he leaned over and whispered in my ear. "I love you."

"I love you too." Our wedding day had been perfect, despite the cold and torrential downpour.

Neither of us had any idea how much work it was going to be for Jason to keep my sanity in the years to come.

***

I have always been fascinated by the brain, for it is where 'we' are located. It is not like other organs that can be replaced and leave us who we always were.

When the brain is damaged all we can do is hope that it will heal, possibly remove the damaged portion and hope it was doing nothing more than disrupting the surrounding tissue and not contributing to our ability to think, process information and maintain our personality. Medical professionals advocate that there is no shame in having an illness that affects the brain, after all you have no more control over that than you do over bone cancer. Someone may be in a car accident and sustain horrendous injuries, broken bones, damage to internal organs and during their recovery they will be applauded for their strength, their tenacity at overcoming their difficulties and their continuing good humour amidst all that pain and suffering. But that same person who sustained an extremely severe traumatic brain injury may become irritable, impulsive, lose motivation and alienate those around them with their actions. Who they were before the accident was the same, but when the brain is damaged it can change everything about who they were and through no fault of their own they will become a person that people pull away from.

It is no surprise that many people when assaulted with depression, neurons misfiring in their brain, don't share that even with those they are close to. Depression does not give them the opportunity to be strong, to keep their good humour, to act in a way that other people will respect and admire them for. So people feel ashamed and keep it private. But the difference is that there is an opportunity for mental illness to be treated and the person returned to who they were, if only they are willing to seek help. It is for this reason that the stigma, the sense of shame and the idea that taking medication to regain your personality makes you weak needs to be challenged.

It is still all too frequent that you hear comments that compound the shame that surrounds depression. People suggest that anti-depressants are a crutch for people who can't cope or that they are a fashion accessary necessary to fit in with the crowd. They ask what the person has to be upset about when they have a good life. There is still a belief that people just need to suck it up, pull their socks up and snap out of it. There is an assumption that we have all been there, with those who haven't been depressed equating their low moments to those of someone with clinical depression. It therefore follows that only the weak and selfish consider suicide, because there is no differentiation granted between sadness and depression.

It is these comments that provided the fuel to finish this book. I want to challenge the stigma that surrounds mental illness, both as a sufferer and as a psychologist. The only way I know to do that is to reveal the most personal, intimate details of my life. These are words that I struggle to say to friends and family, the conversation that I dread. But I will look you squarely in the eye and explain what depression is to me: the challenge of accepting a diagnosis even when you know it's true and the battle with medication. All the thoughts I wish I could convey face to face to explain how I got to where I did. So please, sit down, open your mind and listen to what I have to say, even if at times I struggle to find the words.

Part One

Denial

Are you depressed?

I balanced precariously on the stool pressing the cornice to the ceiling. As a stray hair tickled my face, my fingers slipped and the cornice came crashing down on to my head.

"Ow! That hurt!"

Jason carefully lowered the end he was holding and came to check on me. I looked up at him laughing, before wiping a blob of cornice cement from my nose.

"Not fatal then." He joked tiredly, sweat running down his face.

I gave him a quick kiss before we picked the cornice back up and pressed it into place. Once it was set we stepped back to admire our efforts.

"Perfect! We are absolutely amazing! Best plasterers around!" I glowed, my dark brown eyes shining with pleasure.

"It looks good." he confirmed. "But now it's time for bed."

I shrugged off the suggestion.

"I might start on the flooring." I countered.

"How do you have the stamina to do anymore? I'm exhausted." he asked.

I didn't feel remotely tired tonight and although I had no idea where this sudden burst of energy had come from, I wanted to harness it whilst I could.

"Just keep it down, will you?" He kissed me good night and went to clean himself up.

I began bringing the flooring in from the garage, dancing to the music in my head as Jason slept the night away.

At work the next day my muscles were tight, vibrating with barely contained energy. I flitted between desks, chatting to anyone who was willing to listen. I saw the good in everyone and everything. I flew through my work. Reports seemed to write themselves, and I could answer any question that was asked of me. I interjected my brilliance by helping others whether I was asked or not. I bubbled over with enthusiasm, in awe of the world we live in.

"Can I have some of your happy pills?" My friend asked and I laughed, more than willing to share if only this feeling was from a pill.

For four amazing days I relished the energy and enthusiasm, then on the fifth day I crashed, I burned and I did not make it into work at all.

It was February 25th, 2011. I awoke to a world that overwhelmed me. Our bed was in the living room, the dust from freshly sanded gyprock swirling above my head. I stared at the brown spiderwebbed light shade dangling from the ceiling, suspended by an equally dark, dingy cord and tears seeped from my eyes. Jason was already up and navigating a path around the bathroom sink that sat in the dining room. I struggled to sit up, willing my body to complete the morning ritual. It was too hard, my limbs would not move and my mind was similarly immobile.

I hid away, cowering back under the covers and pretended I was physically unwell. For a day I gave in and hated myself for it.

The next day I wiped the tears away, forced my limbs to move. I dressed mechanically, paying no attention to the items I put on my body. Jason brushed past me, stroking my back, as he reached for his own clothes. I stiffened momentarily before remembering to smile.

"Are you ok?" he asked.

"Of course." I assured him. "I'm feeling much better." I smiled wider, concentrating on bringing the smile to my eyes.

It was a well practiced act. It generally took a couple of weeks for Jason to notice the lack of real enthusiasm and joy, and outside my home I could maintain the façade for months. I was not prepared for someone to notice that the light had faded from my eyes.

I arrived early finding my way to the 14th floor where the training rooms were located. I picked a seat at the side of the room where I could look through the floor to ceiling windows, but still see the speaker. I was attending two days of training as part of my orientation program for my new job. I was dreading this. I'd been warned by those who'd already done the training that it was two days of tedium. Doing it with a friend was the only thing that made it sound bearable. I placed my things over two seats saving a spot for Meredith. I paused, already exhausted. I focussed on breathing, the tightness in my chest making each breath an effort. The room gradually filled up. My phone buzzed with a message from Meredith saying she was running late. I was not particularly surprised. I should have been grateful she was coming at all, but gratitude eluded me.

At my table was another psychologist, an admin worker and two case workers. I kept my eyes downcast to avoid any accidental eye contact and flicked through the stack of notes we had been given. At 9:05 the trainer started the session by explaining the layout of the various offices. I groaned inwardly.

Meredith arrived twenty minutes later. She was my height, but looked taller thanks to her mop of curly black hair and much smaller frame. She was wearing a fashionable dress and high heels, making me feel scruffy in my black pants, t-shirt and flat sensible shoes. She apologised to the trainer before coming to sit beside me.

"Traffic was a nightmare!"

"Glad you made it. I don't think I could cope with this on my own." I whispered back.

My eyes and ears glazed over as the trainer continued her monotone lecture. What a pointless waste of time this was. Time whittled away and I saw no point in anything we learnt. I saw no point in anything. I was so desperate for something to distract me from my self loathing, hateful thoughts, and this training was not going to help with that. I stared out the window, pictured throwing my chair through it to shatter the glass and jumping after it to my death.

After a tedious three hours we were given an hour long lunch break and Meredith and I wandered past the various cafes in Parramatta looking for something to eat. We purchased a couple of kebabs and sat down.

"This is so pointless." I stared at the food in my hand and began to unravel the foil. "Do you think anyone would notice if I just didn't go back?"

She paused, her kebab halfway to her mouth, her head tilted to the side and she looked at me strangely. "What's going on? Has something happened?" She asked.

"No, nothing's happened."

"Are you ok?"

"I'm fine. Really I'm fine. I'm just having an off day." I started eating, turning my eyes away from her.

"No, it's more than that. You're not yourself."

I shrugged, dismissing it. I started eating in earnest, whilst she stopped to look at me properly. She looked at me and saw what other people did not.

"Are you depressed?"

This was new. I was shocked into honesty.

"Yes." Had I acknowledged this to myself yet, or was it this simple question that identified my current state of being?

"How bad is it?"

I shrugged again, uncomfortable with this discussion.

"On a scale of one to ten. Ten is happy. One is so depressed you can't get out of bed."

It's not the descriptions I would have put on the scale. I've never had a depression that renders me bed bound, my lowest points are bound up with suicide. I've heard people say that suicide can happen once someone is feeling better and gains enough energy to kill themselves. I designated this as a two in my head. Which made my worst possible rating a two, things weren't that bad.

"Three"

"That's shit lady."

"Yep, guess it is."

"What does Jason say?"

"He doesn't know. He's in New Zealand at the moment."

"That's right, I forgot. You're heading over there for a long weekend with him, aren't you?"

"I leave on Friday."

"Well, that will be nice." she said.

"Maybe. I'd rather not go."

She took her own anti-depressants out of her handbag and offered the tablets to me jokingly. "Here, maybe you should have one."

"What about you? Where's your mood?" I turned the conversation back to her.

"Probably three as well."

"So we'll be shit together."

"Guess so."

After a pause for eating Meredith returned the conversation to my depression, not able to let it rest yet.

"Have you been to a doctor?"

I shook my head. "No. I don't. I mean, it's not that bad."

"You should. You're not doing well."

"I'm fine really."

She raised her eyebrows in disbelief and looked at me with green eyes that seemed to see straight through me. "No, you're not."

"It usually only lasts a couple of weeks. I can cope."

"You're not suicidal, are you?"

"No." This conversation had already been so uncomfortable and I had never told anyone that I was suicidal. I was too ashamed of that.

"Good. But if you're still depressed in two weeks then you need to go to the doctor."

Back in the office building Meredith decided to demonstrate the stage fighting that she had learnt at her acting class the night before. We stood by the elevator and she fake hit me in the face. I fell to the floor just as the doors opened and a group of people looked at us in surprise. We both burst into a fit of laughter and tried unsuccessfully to explain our behaviour. We followed them back into the room and sat back down. Meredith fixed me with her gaze again. "You have two weeks."

That Friday as I sat in the airport I found myself fervently hoping that my plane would crash. I immediately felt guilty for the thought, as it would kill so many innocent people. But then I rationalised that I had no control over whether or not this plane would crash, it was just if a plane was going to crash I wanted it to be the one I was on.

I had been looking forward to this trip when I booked it a few weeks earlier, but now it just felt like effort. I knew I had to show enjoyment and make Jason's birthday special, there was no reason he needed to know I was depressed yet. I was an expert at forced happiness and together we were experts in denial.

Love is blind

I met Jason when I was in my first year of studying psychology at the University of Sydney. He was in his second year of an engineering degree at the University of New South Wales. Despite doing such different degrees, at different universities, we were certain to meet once my best friend started dating one of his close friends. I had been friends with Clare since we were thirteen and we had spent many hours discussing boys, who we liked and who we didn't. We had even shared a mutual crush on a tour guide when we went on holiday together at fifteen. With over five years of such discussions I was optimistic when she told me she had found a man who would be perfect for me. I pictured dark hair, piercing brown eyes and a slight Spanish accent. Clare and I had both been quite enamoured of Antonio Banderas doing push ups over a bunch of candles in The Mask of Zorro. So when I met this tall, skinny guy with wispy brown hair and hazel eyes, he didn't match the image I had built up. I have always been a sucker for a sexy voice, and Jason's reflected his country upbringing - slightly slow and most definitely Australian. Not my idea of sexy. Given my excessive expectations I really could not help but be disappointed. I had no interest in dating him and Jason, it turned out, felt the same way.

As we spent more time together I began to know him as a kind, generous, intelligent man. He also had a very endearing trait of giving regular massages, a habit that I have encouraged strongly. When it became obvious that we enjoyed each others company Clare resurrected her plan to get us together. We, however, continued to deny any kind of attraction and eventually she gave up on us.

Almost as soon as she did, we started dating. We had organised a trip to the beach with a group of mutual friends. It was the 7th January 2001. Unfortunately, or perhaps fortunately, the day dawned grey and with predictions of rain. All of our friends backed out and it was just Jason and I who went to the beach that day. Details aren't really necessary, but suffice it to say after seven hours at the beach in the rain we were no longer just friends. I remember an awkward phone call from my mother around lunch time asking if I wanted to be picked up as it had just started raining. My rather adamant rejection of her kind offer let her know that something was going on.

The joy of being university students dating in the summer break meant we had an abundance of time to spend together and by the time the semester began we were completely in love. I remember the very moment that I knew I loved him. It was our first Valentine's Day as a couple. He arrived on my doorstep looking his regular scruffy self. His clothes were falling off him, with the mandatory holes and tears and his hair had not seen the benefit of a brush for at least a month. But he held a single long stemmed red rose in his hand and his smile melted my heart. That first year was a time of fun, laughter and sex, with the occasional break for studying.

Jason is by nature stable and not inclined to strong emotions, so he took enjoyment in absorbing my moods, feelings that he could not otherwise access. As I brought him up with my euphoria, he lent me some of his stability, moderating my more reckless impulses. When I felt no need to attend class he travelled across Sydney from his own university to sit with me in lectures, keeping me grounded. Obviously he had his own study to do and could not always be there and I was entirely responsible for my behaviour during exam periods.

During my final exams that year I entered another period of excess: excessive joy, excessive energy, excessive thoughts. My brain was on overdrive. Staccato racing thoughts that stumbled over themselves. They came quick and fast and I couldn't sit still. I left every exam as soon as I was allowed. I finished them all in record time because my brain was at super speed, the answers flowing from me easily. I had better uses for my time than checking my answers, so I left each exam to enjoy the sun outside. In the nights prior to the exams I had not been getting enough sleep and to prevent mid exam sleepiness I drank some coke. As someone who almost never drank soft drinks the subsequent speeding of my mind seemed inextricably linked to this magic elixir. A week or two later when the world slowed down again it was with great anticipation that I purchased another bottle of coke. But, alas, soft drink had not been the cause and could not restore me my endless energy.

After a year of dating Jason and I moved in together. There was no real decision made, no big discussion. We just found ourselves talking about where we would like to live, whether we wanted to share with someone else or just have our own place. We started looking in the paper for rental properties on our meagre budget. We were young and we were happy, but we didn't expect that this relationship would be 'it'. Neither of us were certain that we would survive the changes required to live together, so when we signed our first lease we only signed a six month contract. However, contrary to every bit of folklore we had heard it was not a challenge at all, it just felt natural. Jason was the natural complement to my volatile moods, being a constant, calm, and steadying presence.

It was a stressful year though. I had to write an honours thesis in psychology. As often happens when things get stressful my moods played havoc with my life. Jason was amazing, encouraging me and pushing me to keep going. When the paranoid delusions started he didn't even think them odd.

Bang.

My heart leaps and my eyes dart around the room. They're coming. They're after us. I rush to Jason pulling him into the hallway, turning off lights as we go.

"It was just a car bac..." he starts.

"Shhh! They'll hear you."

I get down on my hands and knees and use our bed to provide cover as I make my way to the window and shut the blinds. One room made safe I creep into the study, turn the computer off and shut those blinds too. The flat plunged into darkness I make my way back to the hallway cowering in the one spot with no line of sight to the windows.

My breathing is still fast, my heartbeat racing in my ears. Sweat starts to dampen my palms as I strain to hear the sounds outside.

Jason pulls me into his arms and holds me.

"It's ok." he whispers "It was just a car back firing."

My wide eyes lock on his his. "Don't talk." I insist.

He envelopes me in his arms, rocking me back and forth waiting for my fear to fade.

In retrospect, it seems amazingly naïve that neither of us thought this behaviour particularly odd or concerning.

✳✳✳

I spent a year working, volunteering and recovering, before I began my doctorate in clinical neuropsychology. Completing my doctorate was by no means a trouble free period, but I was fortunate to have an amazing supervisor. She hounded me, forced me to publish as I went and that, together with Jason's support, got me through. In the few months I had off after submitting and prior to beginning work, I hit another low. This was the first time that Jason and I talked seriously about me seeing a doctor. This was also the first and only time I gave a hint about the seriousness of my depression, telling Jason I was 'dangerously depressed'. He understood this to mean suicidal, but he did not ask any questions, did not push for more information. Neither his training nor his personality had prepared him for dealing with mental illness and he did not know what to do. He didn't think that asking questions or confronting me about suicidal thoughts was the right thing to do. He did not realise that I had spent hours on the roof of our apartment block debating if it was high enough to kill me. One side of the building was on a main road and I thought it would be too distressing for the innocent bystanders who would see my falling, broken body. The other side was landscaped gardens with too many bushes for death to be a certainty. With all the motivation of a suicidally depressed mind I returned to the apartment to stare at nothing, whilst waiting for the pain to pass.

***

The plans for the round the world trip, or as we began to refer to it 'the big trip' had been mulling for awhile. There would be periods when I would go into planning overdrive and set up budgets, design routes and spend hours on travel forums. But it wasn't until I started working full time that we set a date. I was on a twelve month contract and when that ended we would travel. We had hardly increased our spending since the poor student days, aware that this trip was on the horizon, but in 2007 the saving got serious. In one year we saved well over two thirds of our income. We didn't eat out, we didn't watch movies, we didn't buy clothes. Our money was spent on the mortgage and associated bills, transport and the bare minimum on groceries. But a few months before the set departure date the stress of planning sent my mood spiralling down again. I wanted to call off the trip, call off everything. Jason became concerned about my mood and he became more insistent about visiting a doctor.

A bottle of St Johns Wort appeared in the kitchen, a remembered conversation about its effectiveness in treating depression. He didn't push me to take it. I am too stubborn for that to be an effective method. I would pick it up, turn the bottle in my hand, but always put it down unopened.

I was emotionally numb getting on the plane. We arrived into Johannesburg airport exhausted from the fourteen hour flight and jumped into a taxi with no meter or wing mirror. We realised rather belatedly that this was not the correct way to approach travel in South Africa. Our driver proceeded to tell us the stories about when he had been carjacked. The first time he had lost the car, the second time he had killed the thieves, the third time they had taken the wing mirror and meter. Seeing our shocked faces when he casually mentioned killing people he went on to assure us that he was now a good Christian and didn't do that sort of thing anymore. Despite his past, or maybe because of it, he took our safety seriously. He dropped us at our hostel making sure that we were safely inside the barbed wire fenced complex before departing. Having started with a rather black mood, the confined, fearful nature of our first stop made me question all our plans. We had nearly five months ahead of us in Africa, and I had no idea how I was going to cope with it. However, by the time we had made it through Botswana I had fallen in love with the continent and it felt like the months would fly by.

I began to relish the chaos and unpredictability. We became experts at dealing with dodgy money changers, catching local buses and taking risks. There were times of high excitement, constant activities and general exhaustion for Jason. In the space of a few days we walked together with adult lions, flew in a microlight above Victoria Falls, nearly got blown away by the force of the water once we were back on the ground and cheered a labor day parade on it's way. There were other times when I refused to leave our room, unable to cope with anything.

For eighteen months we travelled the globe. We camped in Zambia as hippos kept us awake eating the grass beside our heads, and snorkelled with sea lions in the Galapagos. We ate pho in Vietnam, and walked across the border into Bosnia and Herzegovina for the sole purpose of trying the beer. We explored ancient ruins in Peru, Poland, Cambodia and Ethiopia. We camped, slept in what turned out to be a brothel without a working toilet, and found a bed in a local house when every hotel in town was full. We travelled on bicycle taxis, motorcycles, buses, on the backs of trucks, in trains, boats, canoes and planes.

We immersed ourselves in life and experiences, but eventually we had to return home to jobs, cleaning, the mundane aspects of everyday life and predictably we returned to depression. Not a life changing depression, just another low that passed with time.

Through all of these ups and downs that characterised our life together we maintained a level of denial that was impressive. We did discuss my highs and lows, but never pathologised them. My denial was such a part of me that in my stable moments I managed to forget every previous episode of depression, to the point that even when asked directly I denied ever being depressed.

Prior to going on the 'big trip' we had to get five months worth of anti-malarial tablets. There are a number of possible anti-malarials and I researched them all thoroughly. One, lariam, carries with it the risk of psychosis and is contra-indicated for anyone with a recent history of depression, or a psychiatric disorder. However, it is very effective and you only have to take it once a week, not everyday like the other options. This was the drug the travel doctor wanted to prescribe. I voiced my concerns about the psychiatric side effects, but denied any personal depression when asked. He went on to try and persuade me that it was the best option, and I was at no particular risk. Despite not acknowledging that I have a mental illness I was convinced taking it would not be a good idea and steadfastly refused.

Keeping it in the family

My complete denial of my own mental illness did not start when I met Jason. The roots of my denial began with my family. I grew up in a fairly ordinary English family. A working Dad, a stay at home Mum, two older brothers, a dog and a cat. My earliest memories are snippets of my life in England. Starting preschool and becoming best friends with the girl who was wearing the same blue tracksuit as me. Playing in the little park across the road from where we lived and crawling behind the bushes into what felt like a forest. My childish imagination conjured up worlds that were hidden out of sight of where the adults sat. But in 1987 everything was to change. Unbeknownst to my 6 year old self, life for my parents had become rocky, unstable and it was no longer tenable to remain in our old English terrace house. With a move inevitable the top two contenders were Japan and Australia. I often wonder quite how different my life would have been if I had grown up Japanese, but instead I was soon to become Australian.

We arrived in Australia in November of 1987. I hadn't wanted to move half way around the world, but I had been promised sunshine and hot summers. Instead we arrived to unseasonably wet weather. We were staying in a small two bedroom apartment on the side of a hill. Cars struggled to make it up the street out the front of the building, some being washed backwards by the torrential rain. It was here that I had my seventh birthday. I had no friends and was stuck inside with too many people for such a small apartment. Australia did not make a great first impression.

Luckily we soon found a house and after camping on the floor for weeks our furniture arrived on Christmas Eve. It was one of the best Christmas days I can remember, there was so much to unwrap and these toys and possessions we had been without for months felt new again. Our family gradually settled into the Australian way of life. I made new friends, discovered the joy of pool parties and together we went on long driving holidays out in to the Australian outback.

It's not that my family shied away from discussing mental illness, quite the opposite. My mother was quick to discuss the issues that her brother had faced growing up. My uncle Andrew suffered with bipolar disorder, back when it was known as manic depression and the treatments were less advanced. Following three separate suicide attempts he spent months in a mental institution. Although he was a highly intelligent individual, the medical opinion of the time was that he would never be a functioning member of society, and that his mother should forget about him and leave him in an institution. Luckily for Andrew my grandmother ignored this advice. When I knew him he was successful, working in a job he loved and had moved from being looked after by his mother to looking after her. He was passionate about travel and and once he retired it seemed like he was always exploring one part of the world or another.

I have two older brothers and as each one hit adolescents their mental health deteriorated. They acted out, showing their difficulties in obvious ways. In trying to protect my childhood and innocence the reality of what was happening was not discussed with me. What I heard were the fights, the yelling. I was not part of discussions about depression, or a later diagnosis of bipolar disorder. All I heard was the worry about my brother's drug use, my mother yelling when she discovered him smoking pot in the house. He would go missing and my mother would cry, concerned that he had run into difficulties with some drug he might be experimenting with. I saw the abrupt change in his behaviour, the anger and irritability that was so different from his old self.   I watched in fear as he punched a hole in the wall. With, as yet, no understanding of mental illness I blamed everything that was going on with drugs. At the age of eleven I made the decision that I would never use any drugs. I'm sure that decision made my later battle with mental illness easier.

My parents did not deny my brothers' difficulties, they faced them. By the time I was eleven I had seen two psychiatrists, part of the whole family visit that each psychiatrist wanted. My parents were unimpressed with the first psychiatrist and do not even remember her name. The second psychiatrist is still talked about, and his positive impact still strongly felt. The one time I went to see him I remember being asked questions about what my feelings were being in this volatile house. I don't remember saying much, I certainly wasn't about to open up to a stranger I had only met once. For much of the session I sat in the corridor on a too big chair swinging my legs, feeling left out whilst the rest of the family had conversations I was not privy to.

My mother remembers the summation of my mental health to be along the lines of - she seems fine now, but you'll screw her up later on. What I'm sure the psychiatrist meant was that although I seemed fine, I was at extremely high risk for developing a mental illness considering my genetic loading. I wonder if it was this small comment that prompted my mother to first articulate her need for me to be normal. She became determined to prove this psychiatrist wrong and demonstrate that she could in fact raise a child whose mental health was never in doubt.

In this family characterised by mental illness my role was to be normal. I was the easy child who caused no difficulties. That is not to say I was perfect, but my behaviour was not concerning in the way my brothers' had been. My mother delighted in my normalcy and went to great pains to encourage it. My brothers were acutely aware of their intelligence and my mother didn't want that for her youngest child. I was the unremarkable one, the normal one. It was my role.

As I moved through school taking exams that led me into an Opportunity Class and later into a Selective High School, there was no expectation that I would get in and never much of a celebration when I did. This is not to say that my parents weren't proud of my achievements, they were, but I was always acutely aware that I was not smart in the way my brothers were. The thing I was consistently praised for was being normal. I received praise for not being difficult, for not causing problems. I was praised for not standing out. So this is what I worked for. I worked so hard to be normal.

When my first depression arrived I hid it. I had changed from being a child who loved school, to one who loved nothing. Life became meaningless, but I continued to move through the motions like a robot. I continued to be normal and fulfil my role of being the child who caused few difficulties. My brain had become my enemy telling me of my worthlessness, my inadequacies and my stupidity. My life became unbearable and there was no one I could talk to, because I was normal. I remember one conversation during this time, my mother bringing up the psychiatric prognosis that I would develop a mental illness as a teenager and delighting in the inaccuracy of it. I stared at her incredulously, wondering how she could be so unaware of the truth. I wished for death and for the first time in my life I seriously contemplated suicide. Each day I walked home across a bridge over train tracks. I would stop and wait for the afternoon train, recording the time it went passed. I listened for the sound that it made coming around the corner and how that related to the speed it went under the bridge. Each day I stopped, watched and I debated whether to jump in front of one. I craved death, but stayed alive to avoid causing my mother pain. I was the trouble free child, the normal child. I was constantly reminded that this was my role, that having a normal child gave my mother joy. It wasn't my death that I thought would be the insurmountable torment for her, I had too little self worth to think that I mattered as a person. But I thought the knowledge that I was so depressed and that she didn't in fact have one normal child would destroy her.

Who am I?

Meredith was not a part of this cycle of denial, so she approached my lowered mood in a completely different way. She did not let it sit unnoticed, whilst I tried to tough it out. She continually raised it, monitored my mood and pushed me to see a doctor.

A by-product of our frequent discussions at work, was that I began to discuss it more with Jason.

"Meredith keeps saying I should go to the doctor. Do you think I should?"

He looked at me trying to gauge the correct response. Getting no clues from me, he avoided my eyes. "Yes, I do."

"What can they even do?"

"You won't know until you try."

"Urgh! I don't want to." I knew I sounded like a petulant child, but I had no better argument than this.

"You know I can't make you. But you probably should."

"I'll be told I have bipolar." I tried to show him with my eyes how intolerable that would be.

"What? No you won't. Where does that come from?"

I ran my hands through my hair. It was the first time I'd said it aloud. It was the first time I'd acknowledged it to myself.

35

I have a life-long severe mental illness, one of the biggies; bipolar disorder. It is not all of me, but at times it becomes all-consuming and threatens the very fabric of my existence. It is challenging to define who I am, when who I am changes with the extremes of mood.

I am

goal-driven   motivated
                    adventurous   gutsy
        sociable   loving   caring
    optimistic   forward thinking   in con-
trol
            happy   stubborn   impatient
    a traveller   practical

This is not the first book I have ever written; in fact I have started writing numerous books during my life. Almost inevitably they are started in the middle of the night when sleep feels unnecessary and each time I am convinced this book will be the best of it's kind and win prizes for its brilliance.

I am   **not sleeping**

bursting with creativity

thinking at supersonic speed

FULL OF ENERGY

productive

free with money

good at everything

full of ideas

talkative

FIDGETY

making plans, so many plans

But mania does not last forever, it is inevitable that depression will follow.

I am

overwhelmed by misery
filled with despair
without hope
constantly crying
in pain
not able to take pleasure in anything
not planning for the future
not looking forward to anything
worthless
a burden on others
dead inside
fragile
useless
pathetic

undeserving

finding everything difficult, a monumental effort

tired, exhausted

forcing myself to smile, to laugh

unnoticed

unseen

lost

broken

tormented by suicidal thoughts and images of my death

The mortality rate for bipolar disorder is around fifteen percent and almost fifty percent of those diagnosed will attempt suicide. Yet, suicide continues to be publicly viewed as a choice, an easy way out, an act of cowardice. It is something that you do not talk about, that you cannot admit feeling without people looking at you differently. Even when I told my first psychiatrist the extent of my suicidal thoughts, how close I had come to the edge I saw the shock on her face. I know I present well. I am articulate and have had years of practice at keeping the darkness locked inside, but I was going for help because I was scared that I might not win the fight.

Suicide is not a choice. It is a fight to live and some days that fight is harder than others and some days you just don't have it in you to fight any more. Maybe you get lucky and a friend calls you at the right time, distracts you long enough and reminds you that you will be missed, that things will change and that you should still fight. Maybe you don't. So often you hear people say "I would never do that". What they really mean is "I would never do that in this state of mind." Most people are lucky enough to never get to the state of mind where they may do that. When I am stable I would never do that. I believe I will never do that. But then when it hurts to breathe, when I am crying for no reason except that it hurts - that living hurts, I am not rational and not making logical choices. Irrational thoughts take hold and I believe that my death will cause the people I love less pain than my life. So there is the smallest worm of doubt, that maybe one day I will not be strong enough, not have enough fight in me to believe that this too shall pass.

I was deeply interested in bipolar disorder when I started studying psychology at university. It was a personal interest brought on by my not insignificant family history of mood disorders. But my interest quickly waned as the information I was reading became a little more personal than I had expected or was comfortable with. I had always known I was emotional, moody. I did high on life so goddamn well. The other darker side I kept to myself. But it is a big step from moody to mood disordered. This knowledge sat unacknowledged in the back of my head. The years went by and each time I would enter another bout of depression and consider seeing a doctor that small kernel of knowledge would stop me. I was not ready to hear that I had bipolar. The thought of being treated for depression was

hard enough. I was thirty years old before I was mentally and emotionally capable of hearing the diagnosis,
and willing to seek help the next time I reached the
darkest part of my mind and found suicide prominent in
my thoughts.

The doctor

It was an evening like any other, another Monday heralding the start of another week. I made it home before Jason and collapsed on the sofa. Depression overwhelmed me. Our two dogs jumped up beside me trying to lick my face and I shoved them away, irritated by their pushiness. I turned the TV on, some mindless program that filled the house with sounds. All of a sudden the dogs jumped up and ran to the front door to greet Jason. He shut the door behind him and bent down to stroke the dogs and receive his share of puppy licks.

He looked up from the furry faces. "It's nice to be home!" He came over and started to massage my shoulders.

I shrugged him off and moved away. "Not now."

"How are you feeling?" He asked in seriousness.

"Can we leave it?" His smile dropped away. "I'm sorry, I'm just not in the mood for talking."

"Ok." He sat down beside me, looking at me with concern. "Is there anything I can do for you?"

"No." I just wished he would go away. I felt like he wanted something, something I couldn't give.

"What would you like for dinner?" He tried to start a safe conversation.

"I don't know."

"Do you want to watch a movie or something?"

"I don't know." I couldn't stand it anymore, agitated thoughts that forced me out of the house. "I need a walk."

I shut the door behind me, my keys in my hand. I had planned to walk it off, but the car beckoned dangerously. For a moment I stood filled with indecision as thoughts tumbled through my head, then I jumped into the car and drove away. I paused at the end of the street, faced with a decision that would change my course. Turning left would take me to a cliff from which to jump, turning right would take me to a doctor. Meredith's words ringing in my ears I turned right.

I parked the car at the shopping mall, my heart pounding in my ears as I got out and walked inside. I paced up and down outside the medical centre, but returned to the car to sit in the dark, sobbing.

The next day Jason dropped me off at work as normal. I hadn't told Jason or Meredith what I was planning in case my courage failed me again. I headed down the street past all the business suits hurrying to work and stepped into the medical centre. I took a deep breath as I approached the receptionist and asked to see the first available doctor. She directed me to sit and wait. There were just two other patients waiting, an older man coughing loudly and a mother with a baby on her lap. It was only a couple of minutes before my name was called by a middle aged Indian doctor. He sat me down and asked what he could do for me.

"I'm depressed. I've been depressed for a few weeks now. I have some suicidal thoughts." It came out in a rush, facts with no emotion behind them.

He fidgeted, looking vaguely awkward. This was probably not how he wanted to start his day. "Tell me what happened."

I provided a short history, the high, the depression. He seemed more uncomfortable than me with this conversation. I felt like he'd never had to deal with mental health difficulties.

"What do you do?"

"I'm a Clinical Neuropsychologist."

"Are you married?"

"Yes."

"How is your relationship? Is your husband supportive?"

"It's good, he's very supportive."

"Do you have a suicide plan?"

"No." I was too scared to mention the extent of my suicidal thoughts. I didn't know at what point a decision to send me to hospital would occur and I wanted to avoid that at all costs.

"And your husband knows about your suicidal thoughts?"

"Yes, of course." I didn't mean to give that lie, but it was the answer the doctor wanted. He wanted reassurance I was safe, so I gave it to him.

"You're a psychologist, so you have a lot more experience with this than me. What do you want me to do?" I didn't know, that's why I was there. I was the patient in this office, not the doctor. I wish he hadn't known I was a psychologist, because then maybe he would have discussed things and not assumed I could apply my theoretical understanding to my own situation.

He filled the silence. "I can write you a prescription. Epilim would be the choice given what you've said, not an anti-depressant. Or I can give you a referral to a psychiatrist. What would you like?"

I don't know what I had really hoped from this meeting. If he had offered me an anti-depressant I would probably have taken it. He didn't question me in detail about my symptoms. He never mentioned giving me a diagnosis, neither of us said the words bipolar, mania or hypomania. I knew Epilim was an anti-epileptic medication that is also used as a mood-stabiliser for bipolar disorder. I felt so frustrated with this doctor who felt no need to explain anything to me, or ask more than the basic questions. I didn't want to be coming back to him.

"A referral, I guess."

"You probably know more psychiatrists than me. Is there someone you would like me to refer you to?"

I couldn't believe this. I had spent most of my career working in a children's hospital with children who had brain injuries, learning difficulties or developmental problems. I had recently started a new job working with children who had been abused and were in out of home care. I did not have any knowledge of the adult mental health world. "No."

"Ok." His computer provided him with a number of psychiatrists to choose from and he picked one at random.

I stuffed the referral letter into my bag feeling disappointed and confused. I was no better off than I had been before seeing the doctor. I was now expected to call and make myself an appointment with a psychiatrist. It took a few days for me to muster the courage to make that phone call, and the first available appointment wasn't for another month.

In the four weeks that followed as I waited to see a psychiatrist I had occasional days that I can only describe as dangerously suicidal, but generally I remained slightly above that level at a place where there is the tiniest glimmer of hope, where thoughts of death are constant but you still want to get better and think that maybe it is possible. There were also two weeks of

mania - an amazing blast of light in the middle of darkness.

***

My eyes snapped open and I smiled for no reason. I felt great, yet yesterday I had wanted to die. I
checked the clock and it was only 4:00am. I'd been
asleep for five hours, but I was wide awake and my body
was infused with energy. I rolled over and tried to go
back to sleep, certain I would need more rest to make it
through the day. My brain was filled with thoughts.
What chores needed to be done. What I would do at
work. What I would wear today. A book started to
form in my head. It was up to me to explain this. I
needed to show other people, so that they would understand what it's like to have bipolar disorder. I tried to
shut the thoughts down and go back to sleep. But my
mind was too restless. I slid out of bed trying not to dis-
turb Jason, tiptoed past the sleeping dogs and sat down
at the computer. Thoughts poured out of me on to the
page, characters coming to life. This novel would be a
best seller. It would make everyone understand bipolar
disorder. I would change the world.

Two days later I was at home making use of the
art supplies I had purchased the day before, when I decided I wanted to play the piano. The only problem was
that we didn't have one. The next day at work the idea

popped into my head again whilst I chatted with Meredith. I decided, then and there. I would buy a piano. I excitedly told Meredith about my great idea, my eyes gleaming with excitement.

"Ellen! You're not serious?" As I started packing up my things she threw a book at me. "You don't spend money like this. This is a symptom."

I didn't care, money was not important. An hour later I was the proud new owner of a piano.

Jason was needless to say slightly shocked when the piano appeared in our living room.

"Just how high are you?" He asked.

"Hardly at all." I grinned, and sat down at the piano running my fingers along the keys. "Just enjoying life."

"Well, as long as you're not seeing pink elephants it's all ok." He quipped.

"Nope. Not a pink elephant in sight." I paused, playing a few notes. "Elves don't count, do they?"

"Elves?" He looked at me quizzically, trying to decide if I was being serious. "What sort of elves?"

"Friendly ones!"

"Can you really see elves?"

"Of course not! I just know they're there."

Jason's face moved through concern, confusion and settled on amusement. "I love you."

This was the start of many discussions about the elves with their grey gangly legs, their friendly eyes and their fabulous work ethic. They were my companions, kept me busy when there was too little stimulation outside my head. They danced on the piano and played in the corners of the room. When things got too high and chaotic I was kept awake by them constantly slamming doors inside my head. They were building a castle in my head. They were in my head, but out of it. They were busy doing their own thing, but aware of me when I chose to look at them. I can't make the memories or the visions make sense to me, let alone put words down on paper that will convey the experience.

Much of mania is hard to explain. Things are chaotic, overwhelming, thoughts tumble over themselves to be heard and connections are made where there are none. It is impossible to sit still, because it is impossible to think still. Other people move and speak in slow motion. I find myself interrupting, wanting to hurry them along to get to the next thought. Meetings can become a form of mild torture, the need to sit still, listen and try to follow along with slow ponderous debates.

During this period of mania Meredith and I were flown up to Coffs Harbour to attend a meeting with the team of psychologists who worked in that part of NSW. Together we explained our roles within the organisation and how we could help. Our short part in the meeting concluded, we remained to gain a greater understanding of how this group of psychologists worked. The psychologists kept talking around in circles, whilst my brain raced around the room. I was going mad listening to them. I wanted to scream. I wanted to run out of the room. Instead I took notes. Notes written at supersonic speed, much quicker than the conversation was progressing. It seems highly unlikely that anyone thought my feverish writing related to what was said, but it was the only way to contain my insanity. What follows is an attempt to show the inner thoughts of a manic mind, to show what thoughts a bowl of lollies can precipitate.

'There are hundreds and thousands bouncing off the roof like rainbow coloured rain. Gobstoppers falling on the street and holes in the road. Giant potholes filled with snakes slithering up and out and down the street. Looking for a tree to live in but all the trees are filled already. Goblins and elves have made them their home so there is nowhere to go. The snake finds a rock to hide under, but the ground is shaking and his rock is moving. Before he knows it's lifted up and thrown fetch with gargoyles, or gargoyles playing fetch. Leaping from the tops of buildings down to the ground. Leaping between them, over them. Stone dogs tunnelling under into the catacombs. Skulls lined up in rows, patterns made from femurs and tibias, stars and shields from patellae and metatarsals. Now she's scared and not sure where to go. The lights have gone out and living in the dark where there is only noises. Oozing sensations and where are the slimy monsters? Do you know who you are and what they are? Can you find yourself and decide it's time to climb out of the hole

and see if you can really fly from the rooftops. Flying through clouds but not up near the sun, that's a lesson I learnt before. Icarus, Pythagoras and Homer. Writing an Odyssey or going on an odyssey, a journey, going across the sea. On a yacht all tightly packed and living ship shape, up right, port and starboard. Sailing under the stars, lying on your back in the night. Blackness all around with pinpricks of light in the sky. The stars will lead us to the key so we can follow the worm through the tunnel so fast and so still, so up and so down, spinning in circles but not moving at all. It's like everything and nothing happening all at once. Are you in your body and grounded in reality or floating in space all around your physicality? Consciousness is everywhere so anything is possible all ideas are available and when it's over you can be anything or anyone you want to be. Too many choices and options so it's not a possibility at all. You stay floating everywhere and nowhere. All knowing but not caring. Because all the petty problems, so insignificant. She lost her watch, he stubbed his toe and they are having a very good time. Pause and watch, feel emotions but moving on to watch the ants so focussed and determined or lost and unsure. Trodden on, lifted up. Getting leaves to make a home. Plod, plod, plod, step, step, step in line. Flashes of light and zooming out to see more. A tree filled with life. Bowknuckles playing jacks, dropping the ball bouncing it, throwing the ball. Throwing a punch. Connects! Pain, shooting, up as the skin turns purple. Blood vessels, capillaries breaking under the surface of the skin. Red, purple, yellow, green. Why is it called a black eye? It should be called a rainbow eye. A multitude of colours, a riot like a field of flowers. I see tulips and roses, daisies and lilies. Butterflies floating away and land-ing here and there as a mother comes with a kind hand, a soft word, gentleness within a harsh world.'

So it continued, page after page of incompre-hensible ramblings. My thoughts flying over each oth-er, jumping between ideas without a pause for breath or time to wonder if I made sense anymore.

Meredith and I shared a room that night and as we were getting ready for bed Meredith looked at me with confusion as I put my ipod on my pillow.

"What's that for?"

"It helps me sleep." I wasn't quite sure how to explain this. "Everything is so noisy, and fast. Music gives me something external to try and listen to. Even the fastest beat is slower than my internal world so it helps slow me down, and it drowns out the constant noise."

"That sounds really annoying."

"Oh I don't know. There are some positives to it." To be honest I longed for these times of fast flowing thoughts, productivity, daring, enthusiasm for all that life has to offer. There were admittedly times when it had gone too far and my thoughts had stumbled over themselves in a cacophony of sounds and I had felt scared, confused, agitated and been unable to complete a sentence. But my desire for this state of mind had fu-elled my reluctance towards treatment. It fuelled Jason's too.

I opened the door to the bathroom.

"Hi gorgeous."

Jason heard the question in my voice, wiped water from his eyes and peered at me through the steam. "Yes?"

"I've been thinking."

He sighed.

"I heard that!"

"What have you been thinking?"

"If I could take a pill that stopped my lows, but also stopped my highs, would you want me to take it?"

His head disappeared back into the shower. "I don't know."

I started brushing my teeth whilst he thought about my question. I wasn't currently high or depressed, life was actually fairly stable. I was just curious. We had never really talked about my moods, rarely mentioned the word depression. But we both knew it was there, depression that came in and out of our lives.

He finished his shower and came to give me a kiss, water dripping from his nose onto my face as he leant towards me.

"Ew, you're all wet! Stay away!"

He grabbed me for a bear hug, soaking me with water, both of us dissolving into laughter.

He stepped away looking thoughtful, returning to my question. "I don't think so. I love you. All of you. I love your highs. I'm jealous of them! I love how excited you get, your energy and your enthusiasm for absolutely every-

thing. Life would be much more boring without them. The lows seem fair payment for that. I wouldn't want you to change."

"That's what I thought."

***

I gradually fell from on high and by the date of my first appointment with the psychiatrist I was close to baseline. I arrived at the address, a long brick building with small shabby offices. I entered the closed in room and introduced myself to the receptionist. She gave me paperwork and after I filled it in she glanced down at my occupation.

"Oh, you're a Clinical Neuropsychologist! Do you take private referrals? We have a few clients who could really use an assessment."

"Um, no sorry."

"Oh, that's a shame."

I sat back down, and tried to avoid making eye contact with this chatty receptionist.

After a fairly short wait the psychiatrist appeared down the rickety stairs and invited me up to her office. She had a friendly face, and a slight Polish accent. I sat down on the cushioned chair, sinking lower than comfortable, whilst she sat on her stiff office chair her notepad on her lap.

We went through my history, focusing on the year so far.

"Well. You're a psychologist, so I'm sure you're aware that your diagnosis is bipolar disorder. That won't be a shock."

I nodded. I knew, but surely she could have taken me through it more gently. It's as if she thought my professional background displaced any difficulty that might normally be felt in accepting a diagnosis. She gave me a prescription for the mood-stabiliser Epilim and I was told to return in a month.

***

The night after receiving my diagnosis I organised to meet my mother in the city for dinner. It had only been a few days earlier that she had again told me how proud she was of me for being normal.

My parents were over for dinner at our house, sitting around talking as if nothing was wrong. They did not know I was depressed. They did not know that in a few days I would see a psychiatrist for the first time. I was waiting until then, until I had a definite diagnosis before telling them. I passed my mother the vegetables, the smile plastered on my face. The conversation moved to me, my job, my life.

"We are so proud of you, I'm not sure we tell you that enough." They didn't know. They didn't know the truth or they wouldn't say that. They were proud of my success, my career, my stable happy relationship. Then a word jumped

out and again they said they were so proud to have a NOR-
MAL child.

My smile slipped and Jason's hands clenched in
anger. I didn't hear another word that was said. I wanted
them gone from my house. Jason shook with anger, whilst I
trembled with the knowledge of how much I was failing them.

My palms were sweaty as I walked into the
restaurant to meet her. I was dreading shattering her
image of me. We sat down, made small talk and or-
dered our meals. Then it was time to tackle the issue
and lay my soul bare. I don't know what reaction I was
expecting. Shock. Denial. Concern. I was not expecting a calm acceptance.

"Are you shocked?" I asked, having had little in
the way of response.

"No, it doesn't surprise me. But it can't all be my
fault, some of it has to come from your father."

Part Two

The Descent

Unbearable

Two days later I attended a peer supervision session with the neuropsychologists who I used to work with at the children's hospital. As I was leaving I was called back.

"Ellen, there's something I need to tell you."

I sat back down, this sounded serious.

Her face was full of worry. "It's Mary."

Mary was one of the secretaries who I worked with at the hospital. She was a lovely woman just a few years older than me, with two young children. She also had hydrocephalus, which is a build up of fluid in the brain. This was a condition that she'd had since she was a baby and was controlled with a shunt that diverted the excess fluid into her abdomen.

"There was a blockage in her shunt and she needed surgery to fix it. There was a complication during surgery and she's now in a coma. They aren't sure if she's going to live. I'm sorry."

My reaction was shock and grief, sadness as you might expect. Whether this triggered a new depression or whether I just returned to the depression that had led me to the psychiatrist in the first place is unclear. Whatever happened I found myself sucked to the darkest depths I had known. Light was not only absent but the very thought of light was so very far away I could not imagine it.

It was unbearable.

My plans became specific, concrete and timed. All things that as a psychologist I know make someone a higher suicide risk. I would wait until Sunday when I was supposed to go swimming with Meredith. I would cancel on her, but tell Jason that's where I was going. Then when I didn't make it home he would call her and together they would work it out and at least he would have someone to help him through it.

It was unbearable.

I was unbearable.

All hope, all joy, all reasons for living were absent. I moved. I spoke. I sat. I cried. On Friday I left work to go for a walk. I was agitated, unable to sit still any longer, but there was nowhere I could walk to escape my own mind, my own thoughts. I meandered aimlessly, before finding myself on the rooftop of the nearby mall carpark. I walked to the edge looking down at the concrete below. Almost unconsciously analysing whether it was high enough to kill me. It wasn't.

I returned to work, so confused, lost, alone and without hope. Meredith commented that I was not doing well and I shrugged. She was worried, but she was worried about the coming Monday when I would be home alone, she saw the weekend as safe because Jason would be with me. I left work making sure my desk drawers were unlocked - I would not be coming back.

On Saturday I wrote my final messages of love and apology to Jason.

That night I had a dream. I was lying in my coffin and my friends and family were milling around in the way that people do at funerals. They lined up beside my coffin with trays of food. Each person kept trying to offer me food, whilst telling me that it was better now. That they were better off without me. That I had made the right decision. They whispered these controversial words for my ears alone and I knew these were their true feelings, in stark contrast to what was said aloud.

I woke up early, the remnants of the dream clouding my mind. I knew in some small part of me that it was not what Jason wanted, but in the long run I thought it would be better for him. I watched him still sleeping beside me, peaceful and content in his dreams. "Please forgive me." His nose twitched as it did sometimes in his sleep and though he was deeply asleep, I hoped that on some level he could hear my whispered words.

I kissed him gently awake, ran my hands down the familiar lines of his body. He reached for me still mostly asleep, bringing me close to him. I showed him with my body that I loved him. I wanted this to be his last memory of me. I didn't want him to be left with just the memories of my misery. So I held him close, held back the tears that this would be the last time.

Soon after I left the house Meredith called to find out about swimming. She also asked about my plans for the next day (there were none). How I was going to be safe (I was not going to be). She said things that seem so obvious to any sane mind. She didn't want me to kill myself (are you sure, everyone else does). This too shall pass (but it won't). I did not say anything, did not let her know I was anywhere other than home. I assured her I would be safe on Monday. In some way I meant it too, death seemed the ultimate safety.

In the deepest depths of darkness I forget that this is an illness, that there is treatment or that I would even want treatment. When I am consumed with numbness, pain and taking steps towards ending my life I do not want help. I don't deserve help and I know that things will never change.

I drove my car towards the ocean and parked in an untimed car spot. I wanted to make sure that Jason wouldn't receive a parking fine on top of everything. My mind was chaotic, confused and overwhelmingly black. I left almost everything in the car, the only thing

I took with me was my handbag. I planned to leave it at the top of the cliff marking the spot from which I'd jumped. Inside was Jason's phone number and my driver's license so they'd know who I was and who to call.

I walked all along the fence looking for the perfect spot. A spot with no trees to catch me, no possible ledges to break my fall. I walked through the crowds wondering if anyone else was looking over the fence with the same dark purpose. My tears silently carved a trail down my face, yet no one saw. I returned to a spot early on in my walk. A spot where the waves had worn away the cliff leaving a jutting point with nothing but sea one hundred meters below. All it would take was for me to climb the fence and take three steps and it would all be over. As I stood there staring at the churning sea and crashing waves my mind calmed and I felt at peace. I had expected to feel fear, but I was so unexpectedly calm standing at the precipice of life and death. The knowledge that I really did have the power to live or die helped restore me to my senses. I felt a measure of control that had been absent and was able to hear the words that Meredith had said an hour before. At the time the words had passed me by, not able to penetrate the wall of thoughts that careened around my mind. But now as calmness took over those words nibbled their way into my consciousness. What if she was right?

I did not believe she was, but I decided I could manage to wait. The cliff would be there tomorrow.

Dismissed

A month had past and I returned to the psychiatrist. I told her how close I came to suicide, how unsafe I had been.

"Did you put money in the meter?" She asked with a hint of a smile.

What? I felt she was dismissing it as not serious. "It was an untimed car spot."

"Are you safe now?"

"Yes."

"Well you've had a fairly traumatic month. Let's just leave things as they are and I'll see you in another month."

I was speechless. She had completely ignored the pain I was in, dismissed it as unimportant. As I left her office I was distraught. I started to sob, my tears masked by the falling rain. I felt so lost and alone. The person who should have helped me had ignored me. I lost any respect for her, or belief that she could help me.

I am embarrassed to admit that despite my professional training and my belief that people with bipolar should take medication to correct what is a physiological illness, I continued to resist the idea of medication. With medication came a deadening of the self and a 'cure' for the best that I can be. Without medication I knew that at some point my thoughts would soar, my enthusiasm would be boundless and my energy endless. I would embark on projects I would never consider 'sober', become inspired by ideas that would seem too complex and when I found myself again I would no doubt retain some element of that inspiration and enthusiasm.

I knew that I should continue to take medication, that I should treat what is a medical condition. Sitting alongside in perfect harmony and contradiction was my belief that I was different, I did not need to be treated. That my depressions were not really that bad, that I would never climb over the fence and take those last three steps. It was amazing how quickly the memory faded and I convinced myself that I was never in any danger. That combined with the desire to fly high made me resistant to sticking with my treatment plan. The lure of hypomania is strong. It is a drug that gives an unbelievable high, and I am an addict.

I hated taking Epilim. It left me feeling flat, horrible, not myself. I would wake in the middle of the night my stomach hurting from hunger, even though I had eaten plenty and I saw little benefit in terms of mood.

I rationalised my depression, convinced myself that my job had been the cause. I had started a new job only a few months before this depressive episode had begun and my new office was characterised by bureaucracy, secrets and hostile politics. It was a miserable place to work. I had loved my previous job at the hospital, and had only left as I was in a locum not a permanent position. Luckily for me another locum position had come up. I had been on Epilim for 6 weeks when I returned to my job at the hospital.

It was not difficult to justify stopping medication. I was unconvinced of its effectiveness, had no faith in the psychiatrist who had prescribed it and decided the depression was mostly a result of my working environment. I convinced myself that things would be fine once I went back to work at the hospital. The risk of depression felt worth it, to be myself and to have the chance of flying again. I threw the pills away and cancelled my next appointment with the psychiatrist.

For a few days things were great, my head cleared and I was myself. Normal. It was beautiful. My emotions felt my own again. But it didn't last.

In less than a week I was back in hell. I felt I had to do it alone. To prove that I could overcome my mind and fix myself. If I couldn't then I didn't deserve happiness, didn't deserve to live.

For the second time in a few short months I made specific plans. Exactly one week after I ceased taking Epilim I drove back to the cliff. I spent four hours there, fighting to keep breathing. It seemed harder this time. It was like each time I reached the edge I lost something. Some piece of me was sacrificed to turn away, to go home and to keep on breathing. A piece of my strength, a slice of my hope was left at the bottom of the cliff.

That evening I was supposed to go out with friends, but I couldn't face it. I sent Meredith a text to let her know I wasn't coming, that my mood was too low. She called to check on me, aware of how serious it would have to be for me to back out of social engagements. I told her what had happened, but that I was now safe. I just didn't have it in me to go to the dinner, so we organised to meet the next day instead.

Up to now it had been my choice to share my diagnosis, my depression, my suicidal thoughts. But for whatever reason (fear? worry?) Meredith told the other two that I was suicidal. I do not know what else was said that night. I was never able to ask for more details. When I saw Meredith the next day and she told me what she'd done I was shocked. My first reaction was shock because never before had my trust been broken and I had no idea what it meant. I could not bring myself to be angry with her, but I felt myself curl up inside and I could not face the other two again. I waited, expecting them to contact me to ask how I was doing. But they didn't. I wasn't able to sleep so anxious about what it meant and how it would be if I saw them again. On the second sleepless night I got up and sent an email to explain myself. I don't know if it was a good thing to do, but I needed to face my fear, to give my point of view and open up the lines of communication.

Friends for life

I am not a person who is comfortable keeping secrets, so it was only a matter of time before I started telling friends about my diagnosis. My teenage years were shaped by and large by the school I attended and the friends that I made there. Friends who helped to modulate my moods, who kept me working at least a bit no matter how unnecessary it felt to me. Those friendships have survived through ups and downs, separate career paths and massive distances. These are friends who knew me before I had ever lost my mind, and continued to be my friends even when my grip on reality was tenuous.

It was towards the end of high school that I experienced my first depression, the onset of mental illness. Given the depths of my despair it is amazing that none of my friends noted that anything was wrong, their memories of me are as always being a happy person. I suspect that this is because high school also brought with it my first mania and mania makes me an exhibitionist, in your face and excessive in all respects.

From having no confidence in my abilities I suddenly became a genius. I read physics textbooks for fun, and took over our physics class having decided our teacher was inept. I became excessively enthusiastic about maths concepts, and I was not shy in sharing my inner genius with my friends.

I came up with a theory of consciousness which was going to change how the mind was understood. Based on a manic mind, my theory represented five layers of thought processes. I decided to take one moment and write down every thought I was having at that time. I had made it to one hundred before something else took my attention. My grand theory became just so much paper.

One evening my parents went to a talk by a Clinical Neuropsychologist on stroke. They came back filled with enthusiasm and shared what they had learnt. It resonated with me, an idea took hold and I was going to become a Clinical Neuropsychologist and I was going to cure strokes, dementia, brain injuries! I was going to grow brain tissue. It seemed a relatively simple matter to take stem cells, a mesh of fabric placed in the person's brain and the right combination of chemicals and hormones and brain cells would grow on their own. I would have to conduct research to figure out the right chemicals and hormones, but that would not take long and soon I would be able to regrow a left temporal lobe in a patient following epilepsy surgery!

A friend lent me The Eye of the World, a fantasy book by Robert Jordan. In my mind this became a manual that had been written for me. The characters had access to 'The Source' that lent them magical powers. I followed the instructions each night, doing the exercises to release my own magic. I managed to keep such obvious delusional thinking to myself, but at one point my detachment from reality was revealed due to a hallucination.

It was on a physics excursion to an amusement park. Theoretically we were supposed to be analysing the rides and looking at velocities, the impact of gravity and centrifugal forces. In reality it was a fun day at an amusement park. There was one ride in which you sat on a seat and were lifted high in the air before being dropped and free falling nearly to the ground. Four of us sat in a row nervously waiting for the ride to start, triple checking that our restraints were in place. As the ride started moving up I remember being surprised that my feet were still resting on a metal ledge, I had expected my feet to dangle as surely that would add to the free falling sensation. At the top I looked over and saw my feet on the ledge, felt it, tapped my feet on it. Then we dropped. My heart was in my throat, but god it was fun!!

As we walked away from the ride talking animatedly I made a throwaway comment about the strangeness of there being a ledge. My friends looked at me in confusion. "There was no ledge." But I'd seen it, touched it and could not be convinced. I stubbornly refused to believe that my senses had deceived me and so we all returned to the ride to watch and see if there was indeed a ledge. I was dumbfounded as I watched the ride over and over again rise up into the sky whilst everyone's feet dangled in thin air. It became a running joke with my friends and all these years later they all remember the 'ledge incident'.

**

When I told this group of high school friends about my diagnosis I skipped over the depression. I was in the grip of it and not ready to expose all that depression entailed for me. Instead I talked about mania. As I went through the symptoms of mania they looked at me in confusion. "But, that's just you."

It wasn't that no one had noticed my over excitability, my excessive enthusiasm for things, it was just how I could be at times. I came up with bizarre theories about the existence, or lack thereof, of the world. I tried to explain my universal theories, but ended up casting myself as one friend's imagination. I embraced being different. None of us had the terminology to class my thoughts as delusional or grandiose. I suspect they thought much of my behaviour put on for their benefit, when in reality they modulated my moods and kept me from doing anything too outlandish. At the end of high school in my year book my quote was 'I don't suffer from insanity, I enjoy every minute of it.' The prediction these friends had written for where I would be in ten years. 'Still struggling to convince the world she's sane.' Apparently I had finally failed in that struggle.

***

Not all my close friends were there that night. There were other conversations yet to come. I had organised to meet Jenny to see the World Press Photo exhibition and it seemed like a perfect opportunity to tell her. As I approached the State Library I saw her tall slim figure waving at me from across the road. I crossed the road and gave her a hug.

"Hi chook. How are you?" She asked.

"Good."

"Nice nice." It's Jenny's signature phrase.

We headed inside and up the stairs to view the best press photos of the year. We wandered through each room, occasionally speaking in hushed voices. I caught a glimpse of one photo that showed a man who set himself on fire then jumped off a building to his death. I looked away immediately, but it was all I could see. A shockingly emotive photograph that brought suicide back to prominence in my mind. When Jenny asked what I thought of the exhibit I had nothing to say. All I could remember was that one photo, the colours of the flame and the shape of his body. And just a little touch of jealousy that he was dead.

As we sat on the grass eating lunch I decided it was time to tell her what was going on.

"I have something I need to tell you."

I proceeded to tell her that I was struggling with depression and that I have bipolar disorder. Again I focused on talking about mania. I skirted the topic of depression, and never mentioned suicide. She talked about some of the strategies she had used to cheer herself up when she was feeling low, showing me the list on her phone of the good things in life. She had been struggling to get pregnant and sometimes needed reminding of things that made her happy. There was something in the way she talked about it. I'm not sure what it was, but I had to ask.

"Are you pregnant?"

A little smile. "Yes."

"Congratulations! I'm so happy for you." I said with meaning.

Jenny collected herself. "It's really early though, we only just found out."

Grief as relief

My mood improved slightly, but the depression remained. I was no longer actively suicidal, but neither was I particularly enamoured with the idea of ongoing life. Every day was a struggle. Laughing was a struggle. Smiling when smiled at was a struggle. Getting to work. Getting through each day was a struggle.

It is such a self-absorbed place to be. It seems perverse that when you hate yourself, you find no joy in anything and spend time locked in your own thoughts. Tumbling in circles wanting someone to be interested, but knowing they won't be. Depression is mind-numbingly boring. There is nothing of interest to say, because nothing interests the depressed.

***

My phone rings, it is my mother.
"Hi Mum."
Her voice shakes, her distress palpable without words.
"What's happened Mum? Are you ok?"
"It's Andrew. He's dead. They think it was his heart."

I grieved. I couldn't stop crying. At work they told me to go home, but how could I explain that I come to work no matter what my mood. I grieved and the grief washed the depression away. Grief and depression are such different emotions. Sadness is the common thread but grief does not attack you from within and turn you into your own worst enemy.

Then in the same week my friend died after weeks locked in a coma.

I grieved, became overwhelmed with grief. I was scared; scared it could turn back into depression; scared I could be the cause of grief to people I love. I had to fight with everything I had to keep the depression from returning. I did it properly this time. The first time I had blindly walked into a medical centre, but this time I took the time to find a GP who had an interest in mental illness. My first visit to this new doctor was the morning of my friend's funeral, almost two weeks since the first wave of grief had overcome me. I sat clothed in purple, saying as little as possible because each word brought a tear with it. I started back on medication, this time I was prescribed an anti-depressant and a small dose of an anti-psychotic. On my request I was given a referral for a psychologist. I put on my battle armour, but it was not enough. The grief was already starting to give way to depression, although I was still free of suicidal thinking.

Then the visions came. Intrusive images flashing in my brain.

They started when I was at work assessing a five year old boy. The assessment was to see what supports he would need at school, and with young children it is necessary to maintain lots of energy and enthusiasm to keep them motivated. I clapped and cheered whilst the visions attacked me. Visions in which I stabbed myself in the neck with a knife. I could feel the resistance of my skin as the knife went in. I could feel the warm blood running down my skin. Over and over. All whilst I cheered, kept the little boy happy and interested. As the family left, I shut the door behind them, collapsing against it sobbing. I did not congratulate myself for concentrating past the visions. I berated myself for having them.

I still had no plans to kill myself. But the pictures would come. The elves came back, or maybe they had never left. The castle they were building was mostly complete, but they killed themselves before my eyes. Some hung themselves, others slit their throats. One of my most distressing memories is of the lone surviving elf dragging himself through the blood of his friends reaching towards me with a beseeching hand. I wept for him, a heart wrenching agony because I could do nothing to help.

Inside my head a room filled with blood. So much blood, everywhere I looked was blood. For days the visions were intrusive, not part of me. Subtly, ever so subtly they became part of me and I found myself looking at knives in a way I never had before. Other thoughts started to raise their ugly heads, different ways to escape the pain. The urges that came as I was walking along the road to step in front of a bus. The urges to take every pill in the house and down it with some alcohol, because maybe that would set me free. The medications weren't working. Every previous time I had been here, there was the knowledge that I could seek help, always that bit of hope that help was available if I asked. This time I was asking. I had told people. "I'm depressed and suicidal." I was crying out for help. "I'm depressed and suicidal." I was doing everything I'd been told should help. But it didn't help, so I was losing hope. I was starting to believe I wasn't fixable.

I was just broken.

Making plans

My suicide could never have been classed as impulsive, I had spent too many hours researching, reading journals, thinking of the pros and cons for each possible method. I looked up the anatomy of the neck so I knew where to cut, checking the accuracy of that constant vision. I had no plans to overdose but still I knew the lethal doses for the medication I was on and more specifically which combination would be most successful. I read journal articles documenting the survival of people who had jumped from tremendous heights, so I knew how high it had to be to avoid being a miraculous survival. However, the idea of Jason having to identify a battered, broken body relegated this initial idea to second place, but it was still the only plan I mentioned. It seemed safer somehow as it was at least an hour's journey to the place where I would have jumped.

Most of my research focused on hanging. I learnt how long it takes to lose consciousness. I learnt how long it takes before your muscles start to contract, your brain starting to die. I learnt how much weight is required on the rope to cut the blood flow to your brain. I learnt that even partial hangings can be fatal, that you can die even as some of your body weight rests on the ground.

Until I held a rope in my hands I had forgotten that I knew how to tie a noose. The memory came back of a depressed teenager sitting in a maths class forming and reforming a noose out of a piece of string. Death created in miniature. It was an activity practiced so often it took only seconds to do, even after all these years. But this time it was with a life sized rope.

The noose lay coiled in the bottom of my bag, with me at all times lest it be discovered. I'd tested the rope and knew it would take my weight. I had stood in front of the mirror, the noose around my neck, pulled it tight and watched it dent my skin. I had come so close to the edge, close to dying.

In July I was working at the hospital part time, with two days each week at home. Two days each week with only my own mind for company. Two days each week that no one would miss me for eight hours. I searched our house and yard looking for a suitable spot. I decided that outside was preferable to keep the memories away from the rooms Jason must see and to give him time to call for help and not discover my body himself. The trees were within view of the road which ruled them out and our ceilings were low which was going to make it hard to get the height I needed. There was a beam out the back of our house, exposed and no risk of a hook giving way. I stood on the stool, checked the height that the noose would reach and tried to estimate if my feet would be off the ground. I hung up sheets to hide my body, hide my plans from prying neighbours eyes. I wrote notes to Jason telling him not to open doors, but to call emergency services. I placed them on every door that he must pass through, giving him every opportunity to turn back.

I had done my research and I knew that hanging myself would not be pleasant or easy. So I hatched my plan, using drugs to help me to my death. Not an overdose, just enough to take me to oblivion and as I slipped into sleep my feet would slip off the stool. I stood in the kitchen my box of Seroquel before me. It sent me to sleep each night, but I took no chances. I popped each pill out of the packet until two weeks worth of pretty pink pills sat in a pile, waiting. Alcohol increases the sedative effects, so I poured myself a glass of vodka rather than water. One at a time they went down, until the pills were gone and my glass was empty. Drugs to keep me relaxed, drowsy, unable to save myself. Before they took effect I climbed on the stool, tightened the noose around my neck and waited.

For two hours I stood there, waiting for the familiar sleepiness to hit, but what hit instead was nausea. I cleaned up, removed all traces of what I'd done and lay down cradling my complaining stomach. I climbed out of bed just before Jason walked through the door. He greeted me, kissed me, asked how my day was.

"It was ok, didn't do much."

***

My doctor asked whether anyone at work had noticed, commented. But they hadn't, they never had. I don't know why not. I felt it should have been so obvious to anyone who looked at me. My eyes felt constantly swollen with the pressure of unshed tears. I felt so dead inside, that people should have looked at me in shock that I was still walking around. Jason said I became more vibrant the more depressed I was. He said it was so strange to see as we greeted a friend and my demeanour changed. I was quiet, didn't talk much, but appeared so interested in all they had to say so that even he was fooled into thinking my mood was improved by the social interaction. It was so unconscious, but I did not want to bother anyone with my pain and the more depressed I was the less I wanted to bother anyone. I didn't believe I was worth it.

I found it so hard to believe that anyone would care; that if I put this onto my friends they would still like me and want to be with me. It is one thing to tell someone you have bipolar, it is another to show them what that means.

Clare, one of my best friends, was coming out from Germany. I had a week to wait. I should have been excited, looking forward to seeing her. So how was I supposed to tell her that I didn't know how I was going to survive long enough to see her?

The rope lay curled in my backpack with me each and every day. A week before Clare arrived I attended my peer supervision session as normal and discussed a client I had seen earlier that week. Immediately afterwards I left work - an hour earlier than normal. I walked out into the rain, unable to see how I could live another day. Meredith found out I had left work and tried to call me. I held my phone in my hand as it rang, looked at her name on the screen and knew I couldn't talk to her. She would hear it in my voice. I was still staring at the screen when I received a text message

Why aren't you at work? What's going on?
Nothing.
Please call me.
No, I can't.
Where are you?
Sorry.
You will call me, or I'm calling Jason and letting him know.
Please don't.
You have two minutes until I call him.

My hand shook holding the phone. I was confused and agitated. I knew I didn't want Jason to know. He had no idea how suicidal I was. He wouldn't cope and he was only ten minutes away from me. I could not risk him finding me. I dialled her number.

"Thank you." She said with relief. "I was just about to call him."

I breathed heavily down the phone, big choking breaths as I tried to get oxygen. "Now what?" My voice shook.

"You're really not sounding good. Where are you?" I could hear a level of panic in her voice.

"I can't tell you. I'm sorry I can't."

"Are you near the cliff?"

"No." I could answer that one. I'd forgotten that's where they would think I was. I walked along in silence, making my way into the bush as the rain soaked through my clothes. I looked for somewhere to tie a noose.

"I'm near your work. Tell me where you are and I'll come and pick you up."

"No."

"I'm going to keep driving up and down every street until I find you, so you might as well tell me where you are."

It was such a slow conversation, punctuated by silences as neither of us knew what to say.

"I'm not near a road." I had found somewhere I could tie the noose and I stopped there, sheltering from the rain beneath a tree.

"I'm really concerned. I can hear how agitated you are. What's the nearest road, tell me and I'll meet you there."

"I'm sorry. I'm really sorry."

"You haven't done something, have you?"

"No."

"Promise me. You haven't cut yourself, or taken any pills?"

"I promise. I haven't."

"Thank god." The relief in her voice, but laced with concern for how to make sure I was safe.

Really as soon as she messaged me I was safe. There was no way I could kill myself with her on the phone, I couldn't put that guilt on her. But she made me stay on the phone as I made my way home. At some points the trail was flooded and I had to put the phone away to make my way across. Each time I was given only a minute before I had to call her again, or she would call Jason.

Meredith saved me, kept me alive another day. I was one day closer to seeing Clare. So how could I tell Meredith, Jason or Clare that I wished I had ignored Meredith's texts. I desperately needed to make it through the next six days so that Clare would not fly half way around the world to attend my funeral, but I was not sure how to make it through one day, let alone six. I didn't know how to tell anyone that. I did not tell Meredith how close I was to death. She knew I was distressed and suicidal, but not how close I was walking to the edge. No one knew that I had a suicide plan and a rope that never left my side. I didn't know what they would do if I told them.

What could be done anyway? How can anyone actually help with this? I could be watched constantly, monitored, supervised. But the very thought is so distressing. If I am so useless that I can't keep myself safe, so pathetic that I need to be watched to make it through the next six days then there is no point in being preserved. The idea of asking for help terrifies me, because if I need to then there is really nothing left in me to save.

I hate being this person. There are these short moments when I feel normal, brief interludes of happiness. But always I return to the seventh circle of hell, burning from the inside, suffocating on my own despair. Please let me die. I don't want to have to live through this, don't want to have to survive this. No one should have to cope with so much pain. I have had a good life, I'm glad I lived, but that period is over now. I am broken, a discarded body at the bottom of the cliff. There is nothing left in me to save. Please don't feel bad when I'm dead, I was already broken, useless and empty. I am nothing.

Is it even dying when you're already dead inside?

Searching for joy

My life was not all about death and waiting for medication to save me. I was trying to do other things, to find things that I might enjoy. One thing that I had always loved was acting, an interest acquired whilst helping my mother learn lines for the amateur productions she was part of. I began attending acting classes when I was around eight. The acting school I attended also operated as an agent, and I spent weekends attending auditions for commercials and TV shows. My first pay check came when I was nine years old and I thought myself a professional actor. The highlight of my rather short acting career was a recurring role in E-street; a popular Australian soapie. I remember the first show that aired with me in it and my moment of fame when kids came up to me the next day to ask if I'd been on TV. I was a star!

My moment in the sun was short lived and my character moved away. Although I continued attending auditions for another year or so, I gradually stopped enjoying them. Despite stopping professional acting, I continued to be involved in drama and performing. I did short acting courses during the school holidays and did Drama as an elective for my Higher School Certificate. Once I went to university I stopped performing, although I can't remember why.

In an attempt to find enjoyment I decided to resurrect this passion and enrolled in an acting course. My first class was just after I stopped taking Epilim and I left walking on air. I danced down the streets of the city certain that life was going to improve. By my second class I was back to being depressed and my mood was not changed at all from the class. I persisted though, enrolling in a second course once the first had finished.

During July I received an email inviting people to audition for a Theatresports show. I decided to go for it. I had not done a lot of improvisation, my acting course had been more script based, but I was searching for anything that might improve my mood. At the audition I was the only person there who had come by myself. Most of them had gone through a course learning how to do improvisational theatre together. Actors are in general a welcoming bunch and I was quickly drawn into conversation and made to feel part of the group as we took turns performing on stage.

A few days later I found out I had been cast and my inaugural performance was planned for August 25th.

Beyond repair

Each time I saw the doctor I said the anti-depressant was not working. I was not feeling any better. "I'm still depressed and suicidal. It's not helping." She harked back to a few days after I started on them when I had felt better despite being in the midst of grief. But it was not long before my mood had crashed again and since then there had been no relief. But she persisted and upped the dose again. She told me I was a challenging case and I knew that I was not fixable.

In hindsight I was not fair to her, I did not give her my honesty. I sat in her office, the noose curled in the bag at my feet. "No, I have no plans." I held such a fear of hospital that I could never be honest with the extent of my suicidal thoughts. I never mentioned that I had stood on a stool with the noose around my neck. In my addled brain I could see no reason that these things needed to be said. I told her "I'm depressed and suicidal." I'm a psychologist, and yet when it was me I forgot that there are degrees of depression and levels of suicidality. The rest I didn't say, because I thought it should be known. I never mentioned the visions of the knife. I never explained the utter despair and hopelessness of my mind. Each time I would sit there, saying very little, thinking that she should understand the severity of my depression without words.

87

It had become increasingly easy to say the wrong thing to me, to do the wrong thing. I felt every slight, real or imagined. They cut me deep and reinforced my beliefs that I would not be missed, that secretly everyone would be relieved when I was gone from the world. Not that anyone would say it aloud, because that is politically incorrect, but deep down they would breathe a sigh of relief because they no longer had to deal with me.

I thought sometimes about what people's reactions would be. Not often, usually the thoughts stopped once I was gone. When I did think about it though, I mainly imagined their shock, their surprise. I imagined that they would ask why. I imagined they would wonder how they missed such severe depression. But I did not imagine much grief. I knew intellectually that people would be upset; Jason, my mother, Meredith. But emotionally I did not really believe that it would affect them. They would have a week of sadness, maybe a month, but it would quickly pass and I would be forgotten. I could not imagine that I was worth anyone's tears, that the loss of my life would mean anything. There was such division in me between my intellectual knowledge and my emotional beliefs and it kept getting harder to hold on to the intellectual knowledge. I knew for instance that this would pass, that I would find enjoyment in life again, that this was not just my new state of being, that people would care if I died. But they had become words that washed over me, around me and no matter how much I repeated them to myself I could not make myself believe them anymore.

I feel like I have spent most of this year poised on the edge of the cliff with my body leaning into the wind, as Meredith and Jason hold an arm each and won't let go. Occasionally other people come and hold on to me for a while. They grasp a scrap of cloth, then fade away. Please let me go. Let my suffering be over. Nothing is ever going to change. This is all that's left and I can't do it anymore. I am so unbelievably tired of fighting, of clawing my way through each day. There is no hope left that things will change and you cannot live without hope. I cannot live without hope.

Farewell

August 14th, 2011.

I answered my phone. "Hi Mere."

"Hi miss. Do you mind if we cancel swimming today? I'm in a bit of a state, and need some down time."

"Oh. Ok. Not a problem. I wasn't really in a swimming mood either." As usual she heard what I didn't say, she heard in my voice how badly I was doing.

"I was just going to watch Harry Potter. Do you want me to come over and we can watch it together?"

"Thanks. I'd like that."

Ten minutes later Meredith arrived, looking slightly dishevelled in her baggy red tracksuit pants. She hugged me close, then leant back her eyes searching my face for clues to my state of mind. Jason greeted her from the living room and we went to join him and put the movie on.

I was unable to concentrate, the tears seeping out my eyes. Jason and Meredith laughed at some joke in the movie and looked at each other, then at me.

"Oh chook." Meredith reached out to me and Jason came to sit on my other side. The movie contin-ued in the background forgotten. With their attention my tears sped up. I couldn't talk, so I used sign language to spell my message.

P-L-E-A-S-E L-E-T M-E G-O.

"What is it?" I shook my head. "Please tell me." I couldn't. I spelt it again. Please let me go. Jason knew some sign language, but I was too fast for him. Please let me go. Faster and faster my hands rolled through their message. Pleaseletmego. Pleaseletmego. They asked me to say whatever it was. But these were words I dared not voice lest my intention became clear. It was my final farewell, but she didn't hear the finality in my voice as she left that night.

Suicide attempt.

Suicide attempt.

How can those words be so shocking to hear about myself? I never thought I would have a suicide attempt. I thought I knew enough that if attempted it would be completed.

Suicide attempt. I roll the words around my head and try to attach them to myself. Suicide attempt.

Monday 15th August. I didn't go to work. I stayed home. I was out of hope, out of any belief that things might change. Tired, as well. I was just so tired of having to fight my way through each and every breath. Jason left for work and I lay in bed, breathing, sobbing, struggling to get the energy to do what must be done. There was no point waiting. What point prolonging the agony even for another hour?

I made the noose.

The rope was slightly stretchy. I knew that from when I'd tested it before, but I held on to my knowledge that partial hangings can be fatal. Once again I hung up sheets to hide my body, printed out my suicide note and another more personal message for Jason. I wrote instructions for who would need to be told. I climbed on the stool and tied the noose as high as possible. I stood there for a long while trying to think about Jason, about why I should live. But I could not believe it would matter, that I mattered at all. As I tentatively put my weight on the rope it bit into my skin and hurt. So pathetic when seeking death to care about rope burn on my neck, but I lifted up the collar of my jacket and put the rope on the outside. I thought it would make it easier to stay limp if my feet touched the ground, which I suspected they might. I stepped down off the stool and my feet indeed were on the ground, the rope bit in and I kept my body limp as my vision started to go. Consciousness faded. Then I was standing, clawing at the rope around my neck. Turned out my body wanted to live.

There was a mark around my neck even with the rope padded. I was so angry at myself, angry that I had not let myself go, that I had chickened out. Jason was going to call me at lunchtime, so I waited. I took his call and told him I loved him one last time. Just as I was hanging up, my phone rang again and I answered it without thinking.

"I just wanted to check how you're doing."

"I'm fine, Mum."

"I thought you seemed to be doing better, but when I said so on the weekend you said you weren't." I had been so shocked when she made that comment, shocked by how my outside was at such odds with my internal world even to someone who knew I was struggling with depression. But it was my niece's birthday and not the place for a real discussion.

"I just wasn't having a good day, that's all."

"Are you sure? Is there anything I can do?" I was past that point. I could no longer ask for help, I just wanted to die. My tears rolled silently down my face as I kept my voice steady.

"No, I'm fine. I love you Mum."

"I love you too."

I climbed back onto the stool and shortened the noose to try and keep my feet off the ground this time.

I was hoping that the rope would have stretched to its full extent from the first attempt. It is impossible to describe the emotions, feelings and thoughts that were running through my head, even at the time I doubt I knew. I was shaking, overwhelmed, confused. I had more fear this time. Fear that I might fail again, but maybe this time I would cause myself brain damage. So it was a risk. The chance at death, with the risk being a hypoxic brain injury and ongoing life. It was now or never. I stepped again. The rope angle was better this time, but my feet still reached the ground easily. I looked up at the sky as my head started to feel light headed, like I imagine it would feel when you faint. I tried to concentrate on staying limp, fighting my body's strange desire to live. My vision went black and I was again standing upright.

I failed.

I failed.

I failed.

Frustration, anger, disappointment. I was so angry at myself for not being able to do this thing.

How <u>not</u> to tell someone you tried to kill yourself - version 1

I was curled up on the sofa in a ball, my face pressed into the cushion. The noose was still hanging up outside, but I had failed and still lived to cry another day. I could not bear this pain and there was no plan B, no contingency for failure. I called Meredith, held the phone pressed to my ear. I may have mumbled "Hi", but all she heard was ragged breathing and silent tears.

"Are you ok?"

"No." A quiet sound, muffled by a cushion.

"Are you safe?"

A momentary pause. "Yes."

"Were you safe?"

"No."

"What did you do?"

"I hung myself." I couldn't breath and I was sobbing into the phone.

Her mind raced as to what she should do now. She tried to draw out some details, made sure to keep me on the phone. She wouldn't let me hang up. She figured out the quickest way to get to me. She dropped everything to make sure I would be safe.

She arrived, held me, checked my neck for damage. She took the rope and made it disappear from view. She made me call Jason and tell him to come home.

I do not remember if we talked, or if we sat.

Jason arrived home. Meredith left the room to give Jason and I the time to talk. I have no memory of how I told him. Distress, confusion, chaos. I called Meredith back and the three of us sat together. Hushed voices, lost people, confusion and tears, a river of tears. Pain magnified three fold.

Later I made them read the suicide note. I sat and watched as they read, passing the pages between themselves. It was 5,000 words of my pain. Together they cried and told me they had no idea how bad I truly felt.

I didn't understand. I had said "I'm depressed and suicidal." I thought that said it all.

Faking normal

The next day I went to work as normal, my routine not disrupted simply due to a suicide attempt. I walked through the corridor my eyes downcast as I hurried to the sanctuary of my office. I was inevitably stopped for a greeting, a quick exchange.

"Morning Ellen. How are you?"

"Fine. Yourself?"

"Good. You sound like you've got a sore throat."

My hand flew to the scarf around my neck, a panicked thought that she knew, that she could see it on my face. "Oh. I was off sick yesterday."

"It seems like everyone has a cold at the moment, doesn't it?"

All she thought was that I had a cold. It's not easy to spot, depression. People seem to think that it should be, that you should display the flat affect, the teariness, display all your emotional pain on your face. The signs may be there, but they may be subtle. Once at work I was asked "Are you ok?" and I wondered what she saw. But I was asked in the corridor, so I wasn't sure if she suspected because surely if she did she would have asked in private. Another day and I was asked "What's wrong with you?" when I didn't want to be social. But she didn't ask in any seriousness, did not really think that something was desperately wrong with me.

Both psychologists, both saw something, but neither suspected depression.

I don't think this story conveys how utterly normal my life looked. I smiled, I laughed with friends giving the best acting performance of my life. Unless I told you I was depressed and suicidal you would never have known. There was no one at work who knew, because despite seeing my everyday they had no reason to suspect I was anything other than happy.

With no one at work that knew my story it was up to me to check in with Jason and Meredith every hour and prove I was at work. I had to answer my office phone, or use my office email. I was now on suicide watch and had to be accountable at all times.

How <u>not</u> to tell someone you tried to kill yourself - version 2

Dear Clare,

I am on tenterhooks waiting to find out what happened with the engagement?!??

Things went badly for me after you left... mood went down. Jason and Meredith now have me on suicide watch, which is embarrassing and humiliating and I hate seeing how upset Jason is. Did try and hang myself on Monday though, so can hardly blame them. Stupid stretchy rope. I'm such a screw up.

Hope you are doing infinitely better than me.

Love,

Ellen.

ELLEN NORTHCOTT

Part Three

Rock Bottom

Hospital will cure it

Jason picked me up after work on Wednesday to take me to my scheduled doctor's appointment.

"You don't have to come." I told him.

"Yes, I do."

"What difference does it make, anyway?" He responded with silence. "I just don't see any point in telling her. Nothing has changed."

"You're telling her."

My voice shrank down, quiet words of fear. "I don't want to go to hospital."

"I know. I'll support you staying out of hospital, but she needs to know. It'll be ok."

My insides were filled with fear, anxiety that took over until my entire body trembled. We sat together in silence in the doctor's waiting room. The TV blasting out the evening news. Jason reached over and held my hand, our sweaty palms sticking together. The doctor called my name and we walked in together.

"This is Jason."

"Nice to meet you. Please have a seat."

She took her cue from Jason's presence, guessing that something was afoot. "What's happened?"

I looked down. I looked around. I looked at Jason begging him with my eyes to let me get away with lies, but he gave no such permission. "I tried to kill myself on Monday."

"What did you do?"

I took a deep breath, prepared to tell the shortest version I could. "I hung myself, but the rope stretched. So..." I shrugged. So I was still alive, for what it was worth.

She leant back in her chair, folded her hands in her lap. "Have you thought about hospital?"

"No. I can't." I was adamant, no chance to think.

"It would be the safest place for you right now."

"No."

"Is there someone at home during the day who can watch you and keep you safe?"

"I'm at work during the day."

Her eyebrows rose in shock. "How are you managing?"

"I just do." I had always managed. At school when I was depressed I saw no point in working, and when manic I didn't need to as I was convinced I was more intelligent than the people who had written the text books. But I managed, because I always turned up to school and did what was compulsory. It was the same story in university, there were periods when my ability to study and work hard was limited to say the least, but I always forced myself to do the compulsory work and that was enough for me to manage and make it through. It was the same at work. Meredith frequently told me she was so impressed and that my ability to keep working was an achievement I should be proud of. But I took no pride in it, I felt weak for finding it so difficult.

"We obviously have to do something. I'd like to refer you to a psychiatrist, I think you need more help that I can give you."

I nodded and she turned to her computer to find the phone number she needed. After she had made the phone call she turned back to me. "Your appointment is at 10am on Friday."

I accepted the time meekly, this was not the time to complain about missing work.

Nothing had really changed in my head. I was no worse than I had been the week before but all of a sudden it seemed everyone was worried.

Friday rolled around and it was time for me to meet my new psychiatrist. I was early, my stomach a knot of anxiety as I sat in my car waiting until it was time to go in. The hospital where she worked was in a in the outer suburbs of Sydney, with large expanses of green around the purpose built psychiatric hospital. A single story building full of glass and clean grey lines. I walked through the automatic glass doors onto pale wooden floorboards, a reception desk, more clean lines and blank walls. Directly in front of me were the locked doors to the inpatient area and they seemed to hold my gaze, becoming larger and more important as my fear that I would be behind them increased.

I told the secretary who I was and took a seat, fidgeting nervously whilst I waited for my name to be called. The click of her heels on the floors as she walked out from her office, smartly dressed, asian with short black hair, she looked at me and called my name. I took my seat and handed her the referral letter from the GP. It was a letter full of inaccuracies and misunderstandings. It made it sound like my depression was a result of Andrew's and Mary's deaths, but the grief from their deaths had given me enough of a reprieve from depression to seek the help I already needed.

Again she made me tell her what I had done, saying the words aloud to make them true.

"I hung myself." Maybe she would have been interested in a more in-depth description of the day; the first failure and a second attempt. But I hated talking about all of it. My suicide attempt, my depression, my uselessness.

"Do you feel relief that it didn't work, and you're still alive?"

"No." I felt an intense regret that it failed, an intense regret that I was still alive.

"Ongoing ambivalence." She muttered as she jotted it down on paper. I didn't feel ambivalent, I felt certain that I wanted to be dead.

The psychiatrist continued to go through her long list of questions. "Do you have any delusions?"

"No."

"Delusions like thinking you deserve to die?" I stared blankly back at her and shook my head. I felt so confused, because that wasn't a delusion it was a fact. I always thought of delusions as believing you are God, Jesus or possessing of magical powers. That I deserved to die was not a delusion, it was just a simple fact. I thought that as an intelligent individual I should have been able to think my way out of the hole. I should have been able to conquer my mind. If I couldn't then of course I deserved to die. That was obvious.

"Any hallucinations?"

"No."

I look around the quiet leafy suburban street, my eyes darting around trying to see who is yelling at me. "Fuck off you lazy bitch." Each time I hear him he yells something different. I offend him just by existing as I walk home from work, or walk our dogs around our neighbourhood. But I can never see the owner of this voice, this person who wants me gone and wants me dead.

It never once occurred to me that I couldn't see him because he didn't exist.

This was not just severe depression, this was severe depression with psychotic features. But my psychiatrist didn't know this, because I didn't have the right answers for her questions.

"Have you thought about hospital?"

"I have to go to work. Jason and Meredith are checking on me, and making sure I'm there. As long as I'm at work I'm safe."

"I'm not comfortable with it. You're extremely high risk. A suicide attempt with high intent, high lethality and ongoing ambivalence." She stared me down, making me uncomfortable in her scrutiny.

"I don't have any new plans." I started to plead. The GP had raised hospital as a possibility, but now I sat in front of someone as they considered having me sectioned under the Mental Health Act. I was pleading for my freedom. "I can't go to hospital, I have to keep working. Jason and Meredith can keep me safe."

"I'm not sure I should let you go." We sat in silence as she debated what she should do, and I willed her to let me go.

All my medications were changed, turned on their head. I was taken off the anti-depressant. which was obviously not working, and started on lamotrigine, the mood stabilising drug that had worked successfully for my brother. I was also put on a much higher dose of the anti-psychotic, Seroquel. Lamotrigine would take weeks to take effect, the hope was that Seroquel would take effect almost immediately.

"Ok. I still think you need to be in hospital, but I'm going to let you go. You have to promise to call me or go to hospital if you feel unsafe." Her doubts reflected in her parting words. "I'm putting a great deal of trust in you."

I didn't stop shaking for an hour aware of how close I had come to being an involuntary psychiatric inpatient.

***

Hospital, hospital, they all shout that hospital will cure it all.

Why does no one understand that hospital would kill me? It would kill my sense of self, my independence, my control. My fragile ego would crumple under the humiliation, degradation and embarrassment. There would be no secrets then. I would be unable to return to work, unable to hold my head up and expect anyone to respect me and my opinions. But they are responsible; they have a duty of care and do not wish me to die on their watch.'

There were secrets I had kept to stay out of hospital:

109my intense regret for failing,
my ongoing belief that I deserved to die,
my desire to stay out of hospital fuelled
in part because it would take away any chance to kill myself,

the fact that the only thing keeping my plans at bay was a smidgeon of hope that this change in treatment may provide relief.

Seeking understanding

My brother and his wife had arrived for a two week stay in Sydney. A frantic two weeks visiting all their friends and family. He was the only person in my family that I thought might be able to give me some support. Just weeks before my mother had made a comment to someone that my brother was the one with "real bipolar". She still didn't seem to get it and be able to see through the happy smiling face I did so well, whereas my brother seemed to intuitively understand that just because I looked ok did not mean that I was not experiencing the same emotional turmoil that he himself went through.

"Hey." I answered my phone.

"I'm sorry, we're not going to have a chance to come to your place for dinner."

"I really wanted to talk to you."

"We'll still see you with the whole family, we can catch up then."

"I tried to kill myself. I was nearly sectioned last week." I had wanted to say it face to face but it was the only way to make him understand why I needed to talk to him.

"Oh. What about if I meet you during your lunch break tomorrow?"

"Perfect."

The next day we sat at a cafe eating Thai food, whilst I hoped no one who I knew overheard our frank conversation. He did not minimise or underestimate the extent of my moods. But he also understands that moods in the context of bipolar do not relate to what happens in your life. After we had talked about depression and my suicide attempt he asked how things were going, "you know, excluding that". Although it may seem strange it was not a difficult question to answer. Both my jobs were going well, highly interesting and with great colleagues. The renovation was nearly complete and the house looked amazing. It must seem odd to those who've never had depression, or experienced it only in reaction to difficulties faced in daily life, that I was aware of all the good things in my life yet still suicidally depressed.

The other side

"Here already?" I popped my head into the testing room where Danielle was already setting up for our assessment. She was completing her Doctorate in Clinical Neuropsychology and I was supervising her with the assessment today.

"Just getting organised." She replied with her normal open smile.

I continued down the corridor to my office, retrieved my breakfast from my bag and headed into the kitchen. Soon the smell of raisin toast wafted down the corridor.

"Ellen and her bloody fruit toast!" Max yelled without moving from her desk.

"You miss the smell when I'm not here." I yelled back.

"Hmpf."

Just a normal start to the day. As soon as my toast was done I retreated back into my office, closed my eyes and took a few deep breaths. I could do this, I could get through another day. As I was finishing my breakfast Danielle came in to go through her plan for the assessment.

We went over the patient's medical history, the referral question. It was a complicated case, multiple medical issues, both neurological and physical. Danielle was thoroughly prepared, as normal. I made a few changes to the tests she was planning to administer, and she returned to the testing room.

We had at least half an hour before the assessment was due to start so I started to work on one of my outstanding reports. My chest felt so heavy, and breathing was such an effort. I tried again to get myself under control, but I was losing the fight. I rushed to the bathroom, closing the door behind me just as the tears escaped. I hated being this weak and useless. I was lucky, at least, that I rarely became red eyed and gave away how often I was crying.

I was under control and it was time to pretend to be a complete human being again.

"I was looking for you." I had nearly opened the bathroom door into Danielle. "They're here."

"Alright, let me get my clipboard. I'll leave you to do the interview, just signal me if you want me to jump in at any point."

"Sounds good."

We walked out into the waiting room, called the patient's name and introduced ourselves as we led her and her father to the testing room. The patient was a 17 year old girl who was easily drawn into conversation, talking animatedly about her interests.

During the interview her father mentioned that she had been to a psychiatrist, but that he didn't know why. She had refused to elaborate in front of him, so I took over the interview once he left the room.

"We're just going to ask you a few more questions now your Dad's out of the room. Anything you tell us we can keep confidential if you request, unless it is something that could cause harm to you or someone else. In those cases we will have to break confidentiality, but we'll talk about it with you first. Do you understand?"

She nods back. "Yes."

"Good. Can you tell me why you were referred to a psychiatrist?"

Her happy, animated face was passive for a moment. "I tried to kill myself."

I had rarely had to do suicide risk assessments, and it was not something that we learnt specifically during my degree. But this year I had observed innumerable suicide risk assessments, done by GPs, Psychiatrists and Psychologists. I had seen different approaches and methods. As these were all done on me, I knew which led to my most honest responses, but I also knew if she didn't want me to know there was no question that would get the honest answer.

I was straightforward and direct. I did not lower my voice, or change my tone in anyway. Suicide is not shocking, it is just another topic that we would talk about. We discussed exactly what the suicide attempt involved, when it was, how far it went, what happened afterwards. Then we moved onto current thoughts. I didn't make this into a big deal, the switch from past to present, it was a natural progression of the conversation.

"Do you still want to die?"

She nodded. She didn't look comfortable talking about it, but very few people are. It took trust for her to tell us what was going on.

"Do you have thoughts about hurting yourself?" Is it a passive desire to be dead, or an active desire to kill yourself.

"Have you thought about what you would do?" Do you have a plan?

"Do you have access to any medication?" Do you have the means to carry out your plan?

"Have you thought about a time or place?" How specific is the plan?

Her plan was vague and unspecific. She backtracked slightly, there was an ambivalence about living or dying. The suicide attempt she mentioned was a while ago, and was aborted before it was started. Some pills in her possession, but not yet taken.

I was on the other side of this suicide risk assessment from what I was used to, and I had to calculate the risk. She didn't seem high risk to me, but neither was I comfortable doing nothing. She had a mental health team who were involved, a counsellor and a psychiatrist she had seen once. I decided that we should tell her father, before he took her home and let the counsellor and psychiatrist know what she had told us.

I wanted to check that my own level of suicidality was not influencing my decisions in this case. It had only been one week since I had hung myself, and I desperately wished I was dead. I had a plan, but not yet a time, nor had I obtained the means. I should, by rights, have been in hospital. It seemed hypocritical of me to go against this girl's wishes so I could keep her safe, but I had to detach the depressed and suicidal me, from the me who was this girl's psychologist. Whilst Danielle conducted the neuropsychological assessment I checked with the Clinical Psychologist who worked in my department. I grabbed her in the corridor, ran through what I'd been told and what my decisions were. It was ultimately my call, but she thought what I'd said seemed reasonable.

After Danielle concluded the testing it was time to return to the earlier discussion.

"I'm worried about what you've told me regarding your suicide attempt, and the fact that you're still feeling suicidal. I think that your Dad needs to know what's going on, before you go home, so that he can help keep you safe."

She backtracked, side stepped, argued her way to keep her secret.

"My mother knows. The psychiatrist knows. The school counsellor knows."

ELLEN NORTHCOTT

"But they aren't here, and I need to know that your Dad knows before you go home with him."

She refused to sit in the room whilst we told her father. It turned out he already suspected and was keeping the medication locked up at home. She left angry at me, but she was safe and would get the help she needed.

After they left I sat with Danielle. A tear rolled down her cheek. It's emotional, suicide.

"Is that the first suicidal client you've seen?"

"No, I saw one on my first placement."

"Are you ok?"

"I'm ok."

"I'm here if you need to talk about it."

I felt strangely detached from it. Suicide had lost the ability to be shocking, in me or someone else. I kept running it over in my mind, checking again and again that I was not minimising her suicide risk, by comparing it with my own. A few days later at peer supervision Danielle and I presented the case, to discuss not just the cognitive results, but also the decision making process with suicide risk assessments.

The discussion got passionate with a general frustration at the limited amount of training students have in this area, given the importance of the skill. It should come naturally. There is no chance to get a checklist or a cheat sheet to conduct the assessment. The more stilted and formal it becomes, the harder it is to maintain a good rapport and extract truthful answers.

Temporary joy

I arrived at the Roxbury Hotel in Glebe early to grab a bite to eat. I recognised some people from the audition and they waved me over. Once we had eaten some food we headed upstairs to the theatre. It was a small room and we started by setting up the seats for the night. We put out about sixty chairs facing the stage, hoping we would fill them. The host for the night, Marco, arrived and we took our seats whilst he explained the format and rules. Then it was time for the warm up.

"Make a shape with your body." Marco said. Everyone moved and froze in various positions.

"Another shape." A myriad of movements.

"And another." I started to wonder how I was supposed to think of more positions as we were told again and again to create new shapes.

Marco touched one person on the shoulder. "You stay like that. The rest of you relax. Now someone start a scene with him based on the shape of his body." A scene about a tug-of-war game began. "Pause." Marco interrupted. "Someone else go in and start a different scene based on their current positions."

So the warm up continued until all sixteen of us were joined in a giant scene.

Marco then got us up on stage. "Four people on stage." Everyone was eager and six people ran towards the stage, two returned to their seats. "I want to see a love-in-a-minute scene. For those that don't know, you have sixty seconds before someone has to say 'I love you.' But it has to be said with feeling. It will be set in a hair dresser and you must use a golf club. Go"

As soon as they were off stage another three people got up. "This time I want to see a sit-stand-lie scene. So one person must be sitting, one person standing and one person lying down at all times. Suggestions from the audience for a profession, location and emotion."

We continued to play with scenes, which was particularly helpful for me as I didn't know the rules for any of the games. By the time the show started I was feeling the best I had in a long time. A group of people had come from work, as well as my parents and other friends. In total sixteen people came to see me perform.

The doors opened at 7:45pm and the room gradually filled up and it started to hit home that all of these people were paying to see me on stage. We had to find extra seats because more people had come than we expected. It was a heady mixture of excitement and nerves. The lights were dimmed and the room descended into darkness. The show was about to start. My favourite scene of the night was an emotion replay. We performed a short scene in a classroom, one person

becoming the teacher and three of us becoming students. We then had to perform the same scene with
ecstasy, with paranoia and with grief.   I was in the moment, and felt free.

Knife's edge

Burnt.
    Broken.
        Failing.
            Falling.

Help. Someone please help me.

Destroyed.
    Empty.
        Scared.

Scared to drop again. This was probably when I was supposed to call my psychiatrist or psychologist and ask for help. But that scared me too. I saw that as weakness, and I was already so weak. Fragile. Crumbling into nothing. There was so little left of me, that I couldn't cope with anything. I sat at my desk feeling pathetic, useless and incompetent. My office door was open, but I was unable to move from my computer to shut it, because the tears wouldn't stop rolling down my cheeks and I was terrified that someone would see and ask what was wrong. There was nothing wrong except me. Except my useless, broken mind that couldn't hold on to any positive emotions, but relished the misery and pain. It felt so much harder after a moment of normality. That moment last night when I felt enjoyment on stage. But it was so brief, such a small moment of joy and to lose that again and find myself back in the darkness was unbelievably painful. I heard laughter outside my office and felt so disconnected from it. Trapped. It was so disheartening and soul destroying to realise that things were not improving; that things would never improve.

The hopelessness was threatening to overwhelm me. I knew that was dangerous. I knew I needed to hold on with all my might to some sliver of hope, but I didn't know how.

I had not bought another rope since the other one was taken from me.

I will fight. I will fight. I will fight. I will breathe. If I can manage nothing else I will fight to breathe.

But I could feel my hope, my strength, my will being sucked out of me into the black hole. I would try and think a positive thought and see it swallowed by the darkness before it was able to register at all.

Please forgive me for my weakness, forgive me for my stubbornness, forgive me if I can fight no longer.

I was teetering on the edge of ambivalence, so unsure if I should tell someone. If I told Jason then I would be watched and probably be kept safe. If I told the mental health professionals I may have found my options even more restricted. But I did not know if I wanted to be kept safe. I did not know yet which way I would fall from this knife's edge I walked. I did not know if I would find myself tomorrow wanting to live or wanting so desperately to die. I thought most likely that this ambivalence would persist and I would stay stuck in limbo, unable to die but hardly living either.

It's a weird thing to think of your own death. To know that with one action you could cease to exist. You will not see the reactions, you will not know if people cared and wish they could have helped you in some way. You will not see the sighs of relief. There is no pleasure in death. There is a nothingness. It is hard to imagine. We are so attached to our own cognitions that the very idea that they will be no more is odd, foreign and strange. There will be no guilt. There will be no regrets. There will be no possibilities. I understand why people believe in religion, because without religion you have to face the fact that when your body dies there is nothing. It is not even that the thought is disturbing or distressing, but more that it is odd. I struggle to get my head around the idea of nothing. You can't visualise nothing. You can't describe nothing. I had accepted death as inevitable, but despite what I thought it was not something I wanted. You can't want nothing. You can want to escape from unbearable torment and agony, but that is not the same as wanting nothing. I thought

of those I knew who had died and they were not nothing. They were an amalgamation of memories and stories. They live on for a little while, another lifetime,
because the survivors remember them. But when I died
I would be nothing. Odd. I wanted to die, but intellectually that made no sense. I had no answer for this co-
nundrum, but it intrigued me. Always the intellectual
side of me intervenes, takes my strongest emotions and
breaks them down to understand them.

***

I had not worked out a new plan, but still my
mind worried and gnawed at thoughts of how to get the
rope high enough. I knew I needed my feet off the
ground, that I did not have it in me to keep my body
limp for long enough to lose consciousness. I was only
booking in patients a week in advance or maybe two, in
case I died before I had a chance to see them. I didn't
want to disrupt my workplace too much and in my broken mind I felt my death would only be an inconve-
nience due to the disruption to patient care. I didn't
think it would matter apart from that.

I made myself a deadline for the coming weekend, so that my brother and his wife who were visiting
from England did not have to fly back for my funeral,
but could just change their tickets. However I would
wait until the photoshoot that my mother had planned,

as she was so excited at having photos of the whole family together. That seemed the best way to avoid inconveniencing people by dying.

I knew if I voiced those thoughts I would be in hospital before I could count to ten. I did not really think I was likely to make another attempt, but the thoughts were still there and I knew from previous experience that the step to being truly suicidal was a small one that could happen quickly and without warning.

I was asked by my psychologist what would be worse, death or hospital? That was a no brainer, hospital. Death would be welcome.

That afternoon I went home via the hardware store. I stood in front of a myriad of ropes, examining each for strength and stretch. The one I chose was white with blue specks, the sales assistant smiled as she sold it to me.

It will hurt

Time moves excruciatingly slowly when depression is everything. There is nothing to distract and help speed time on its way. Things had deteriorated again, that smidgeon of hope that the new medication may help dwindled. I had only been on the new medication for one week when I purchased a new rope. That week felt like an eternity.

This rope was rated for 350kg and low stretch. It was thinner than the first. A rope that would cut into my neck; in my head I saw the photo in a journal of a bloody neck after a girl hung herself with shoelaces. There was no opportunity for a second failure. I would make sure to keep my feet off the ground. I knew it would hurt and it is a horrible sensation as the blood stops flowing to your head. I had no romantic delusions about what death would be.

It will hurt. I will hate it. I will suffer. I deserve to.

This became a mantra in my head. Over and over it played for days.

It will hurt. I will hate it. I will suffer. I deserve to.

I wrote reports, made conversation, read a book. But over and over a constant undercurrent of thought tormented me.

It will hurt. I will hate it. I will suffer. I deserve to.

It was accompanied by visions of the stool, the rope, myself stepping into oblivion. I choked, I struggled, I changed my mind, but there was no option to go back. It was to be my punishment for being who I was, my punishment for being weak, my punishment for being selfish.

I looked back at everything I'd written, back at the beginning of the year when I was scared I would not win the fight to live, but losing no longer scared me. I had fought. I did not give up the day the ground gave way beneath me; I did not succumb to the first suicidal impulse. I had fought, but I no longer believed that fighting would help. I could not see this condition as temporary. I had a lifelong severe mental illness that had got steadily worse over time. I had been unable to conquer it with love, with simple pleasures or even with intellectual critique.

I wished I had succeeded the first time around, because since then I felt like each day had reinforced my uselessness, my ineptitude and my weakness. I was coping less and less. It felt like the very effort involved in forming a sentence was beyond me. My façade was crumbling. I was spending hours each day at work weeping, unable to keep it inside any longer. Hours with my door shut, writing reports as tears blurred my vision. There was no relief, no break from the agony and it was too much for me to bear.

I believed the treatment, the medications could get me to survive in life, to function, turn up to work and go home, but I couldn't see a future that held any enjoyment or pleasure. Life was meaningless. When I talked to my brother he made a comment that other people think about me so much less than I think they do, but I knew they didn't think about me at all. You only think about people who matter and I mattered not at all.

I didn't know how to ask for help. I kept being told that I should tell someone when I didn't feel safe, but it seemed so manipulative. If I could tell someone that I was not safe then I would be admitting that I didn't want to die, which meant I was safe and not in need of help. It seemed to me that it was just a way of testing whether people would drop everything for me, a way of testing how much people cared. That didn't seem fair. If I had reached the point of no return where I was truly unsafe then I wouldn't tell, because at that point I don't want to be stopped.

There were things I wanted to say, my final words.

I know I have been blessed by the friends I have had in my life. Not one friend on hearing I have bipolar, hearing about the depths of my depression and the suicide attempt has pulled away. I think that says a lot. For those that knew the truth and those that didn't I am sorry to touch your life with death. Please do not feel guilt for that is the last thing I want anyone to feel.

For those people who saw me every day and did not see at all; it was my choice to keep it to myself. It was the way I always dealt with it and it allowed me to keep functioning. Even though this year was so much worse I do not think I would have let you in even had you asked directly, because I was too ashamed and too afraid to lose professional respect. I debated being open, to help to fight the stigma that surrounds mental illness, but I lacked the courage for such a step.

I am no longer ambivalent. I want to die. No uncertainty, no second chances. Please don't mourn me. It was up to me to reach out for help when I needed it, but all the help that is left is help to keep me alive, not help to make me better. I have nothing left. It has been eight solid months of hell and I am done. I am done fighting. I am done. I am sorry, but it is better this way. You would not have liked the person I am becoming. There is nothing good about this person. Hate me. Despise me. Get angry at me. I deserve it. This was a selfish act. I know that. Do not forgive me. Just forget me. Forget me, so that I can disappear from the world and leave no mark of my pain behind. Fade me out of photographs and erase me from your hearts and minds. I have been dead so long and nobody has been able to resuscitate me, so it's time to call it. Hear that doctor, call it. Time of death. Let me go.

The constant monitoring had faded somewhat, although I still had to check in a couple of times a day. My third appointment with my psychiatrist was approaching. There was a window of hours when no one knew where I should be. The appointment was at 8am and Jason didn't know what time I would make it to work. I had no intention of making it to work after that appointment.

The night before the appointment Jason decided he wanted to come with me to see the psychiatrist. I was scared of what he might say. He knew how broken I still was, that nothing had improved since the suicide attempt. I was brutal and cruel. I wanted to hurt him so he would want me dead. I wanted to scare him so he would say nothing. I explained in detail how I would kill myself if he put me in hospital, or alternatively that I would talk my way out just so I could die. I believed it, so I made him believe it too. In my head I believed that if I was hospitalised that my friends would abandon me and my career would be over. We talked and cried together as I tried to make him see how painful my world had become and that granting me death would be merciful. His tears and pain across his face as he denied my words, refused to do anything but love me.

"I can't promise to be alive in a week." I was brutally truthful, whilst denying him any opportunity to try and save me. I was cruel.

I could not convince him out of coming so I had to reassess my plans. He was going to drop me at work after the appointment which meant he would feel safe that I was there. I would still have a window of time, although less than I'd hoped. I would just have to be quick.

That morning as we sat in the psychiatrist's office he said nothing and I said very little.

"Do you have any current plans?"

"No."

She rephrased her question. "How would you kill yourself?"

Denying knowing such a thing would have been fake, so I minimised instead. Threw the same two plans in the air casually. Hanging, jumping off a cliff. Either one. I gave her no hint that I planned to die that morning within hours of leaving her room.

Jason dropped me at work and I waited until he was out of sight before calling in sick and walking back home. This time I hung the noose inside. The rope was white with blue flecks. Hung above our sofa which is a rich red. The blue curtains shut behind me. Strong colours that would come flooding back in later visions. I had the height I needed here with a rope that would not stretch. But as I stood there on the stool all I could see was Jason's pain filled face the night before and his inability to understand why I deserved to die. Tears ran in rivers down my face, but I could not take that step. I loved him too much to do that, and I hated him for stopping me. I did let the noose take some of my weight, a kind of Russian roulette because if I waited too long I would die.

The police

Two days later I was supposed to go to dinner with friends, but I cancelled. It was another chance to be out of contact, another window of time when Jason would think he knew where I was. I do not know if I planned to die that night, but I wanted the opportunity. I wanted to go back to the cliff, to stand on the edge and debate my options. Meredith found out I had cancelled, knew that meant I was doing badly. She called me on Thursday evening. Jason was there watching the phone ring and questioning why I wasn't answering. So to stop his questions I took the call. I didn't want to take the call. I didn't want to be asked my plans. But I took the call.

Meredith offered to pick me up from work, drive me to dinner on Friday, drive me home again, but I couldn't face being social. It is ridiculous to try and have a conversation when I am that close to the edge, when my mind is full of agitation and I can see no way to live another day. So after work on Friday I went home.

I was distraught. I was agitated. I jumped in the car and drove off into the night, leaving my phone at home, purposefully leaving my phone at home so no one could talk me down.

Jason arrives home and the car is not in the driveway. His heart drops, his worst fear is here. He comes inside and rings my phone, he hears it in the living room and panic sets in.

Tears were streaming down my face. I parked the car outside the hospital where I worked. I tried to collect myself, but my internal world was so chaotic. I knew I had to call Jason. Even in my confused state I knew that Meredith would have let him know I was not going to dinner.

He dials 000. A surreal world where he must report his wife as missing, when she's been out of contact for only one hour. It is a perfunctory conversation. Why he is concerned. Where I might be. The details of the car I'm driving. Police are dispatched to my likely location, and to the house to get more details.

I walked towards my office, through the strangely quiet halls of a hospital at night. I was hoping that no one would be in the department, still working at 7pm on a Friday. I unlocked the door and stepped into the darkened corridor. I walked past each closed office and breathed a sigh of relief that everyone had gone home for the weekend.

The police are taking my history from him, my suicide risk, my plans, any clues to how they can find me. He gives them a photo from our wedding day, and promises to email a more recent one, when the phone rings.

I called to say I was sorry. I called to say I loved him. The police were at our house, I could hear them talking in the background. I was terrified. I refused to let him know where I was. Confused, agitated, rational thought too far away for comfort. I could not get back in the car. I was so scared of being caught by the police, like an errant child told off for running away. In a moment of sanity some weeks ago I had told him of the cliff I had found, the cliff that had the potential to kill me. He told me the police were there already. I hung up, his fear in my ears, my fear fighting its way to prominence above the anger for my thwarted plans. Anger at having death made harder to attain, fear of policeman waiting to take me to hospital.

As he hangs up from our short conversation they ask whether I am coming home. He doesn't know. He thinks I will, but he doesn't know.

I sat in the darkness crying and crying and crying. It is this agitated depression that is so dangerous, a depression that cannot be made stationary, that cannot be born in stillness. It is this agitated depression that takes away my ability to think clearly, so I sat transfixed unable to think my way through the maze of options before me. The options to live or die, to run away and disappear, but never the option for hospital.

They ask if he needs someone to talk to, whether he needs a counsellor. He declines the offer, but is touched by how much they care. They say to call him if I come home, that they will keep looking until then. They leave him alone with his fear, as he waits for the phone to ring.

I called Jason again, his fear and mine bouncing off each other. He assured me that he had sent the police away and that once I got home he would call the police and it would go down as an anxious husband. I was so angry with him when I got home, so angry at him for keeping me here when all I wanted to do was die. He apologised, apologised for calling the police not yet aware that in doing so he may well have saved my life.

Part Four

Once the crisis had passed

Limbo

You get desensitised to it: depression, suicide. It doesn't make it easier, it doesn't make it hurt less. But you forget there is another way to feel. The day my mood crashes I break down, I cry, I want to scream and rally against the unfairness of it all. Then I accept it. This is how it is. There is no other way to feel. As my mood started to creep back towards the light after so long in the dark I was untrusting. I had learnt not to hope too soon. There were four days where I didn't see it. Four days when I didn't have a single vision of my body hanging from the noose. Not one. But they returned and everywhere I looked I saw my body. I saw the noose. My brain desensitising me so that when it was real it wouldn't be scary. I didn't even rate that as severe depression. I knew there was worse. I had lost all perspective on what normal is, on what it feels like to be normal.

In those four days there were moments, fleeting moments, when I thought that maybe I might get to a place where I would be thankful to those who saved me over and over. I was not glad to be alive, still could not see it would have been a bad thing if I died, but I could catch a glimpse of a place where I might be glad. I even saw a little way into the future. But then the visions came back and I could only see one day at a time.

As my mood crept up again I started questioning whether I was still depressed. I felt so much better than I had for so long that I wondered if this was baseline, if this was what it used to feel like before the depression kicked in. But I was not making plans. I was not looking forward to the future. I was still ambivalent about whether I lived or died. I could not in any honesty thank those people who had saved my life. Yet it was the best I'd felt in a long time. I smiled occasionally even when no one was looking. I only had the suicidal images and thoughts a couple of times an hour. I didn't have to see my body hanging from the noose everywhere I looked; all day, every day. I was not curled in a ball crying as soon as I got home from work. These may sound like small things, but it was so much less tiring to keep breathing.

I wanted to ask other people whether they were glad to be alive, whether they really want to live a long life. For me the idea of a long life was in and of itself depressing. I filled in a depression questionnaire and tallied up my answers. I still rated in the severely depressed range, but this was mild. This was such a mild level of depression for me.

One day at work a fellow neuropsychologist was scoring this particular questionnaire that a patient had completed. She turned to me.

"He has said that he feels life is meaningless most of the time. The poor kid, that's so sad!"

I looked over at the questionnaire that she was scoring, a barrage of marks that represented the level of emotional pain that this child felt.

"Yes, it is." But life was meaningless. How did she not know that this applied to me all the time.

I was in limbo.

I was waiting.

As my mood improved I found myself fervently hoping it was due to the medication. Six months ago I would have been wishing it was my own mind recovering, now I longed for medication induced stability. I knew I would not survive another crash if it came soon. I needed a break, a break that was measured in months not days.

One step up, two steps down

The emptiness consumes me. The hollowness envelopes me. I shrink inside my shell and hide from the world.

I understand why they call partners, friends and a career protective factors because without them there would have been no reason to fight. It was the threat of other people's pain that kept me dwelling in my own.

What they don't say in the research is how much the suicidal mind resents those protective factors. I did not want to be protected from death, I wanted to be protected from pain. Those supposed protective factors kept me in pain, forced me to continue fighting to breathe no matter how much it hurt. It circled viciously as I hated myself for resenting them for loving me, when all they wanted was for me to remember how to love myself. I felt so unworthy of their love, of anyone's love. I learnt to cry silently, to swallow the sobs that overwhelmed me so that Jason didn't have to deal with my pain anymore. I didn't want anyone to know that I was sinking again.

I went to work, smiled, made jokes. I talked with conviction about my client's needs, the research that is needed. I volunteered to take on tasks. I appeared in control, happy, knowledgeable. Then I went home and hid in the darkness, hoping my husband would not notice that I couldn't keep the tears in anymore. I cried my tears, expelled the darkness with my words, until I found the strength to go to him, to smile again, to show the happiness I knew he needed to see.

What life is that? I used to work so I could afford the time at home, the life that happens outside. But my life was not worth working for, outside work I was overwhelmed, swamped with misery. I hated it. I hated me. I hated that I was so self-pitying. I hated that I couldn't be happy.

Each night the same scene played itself out. Jason in the living room playing with the dogs, reading a book or watching TV. Me behind closed doors, sitting in the dark, my face illuminated by the computer screen as it waited for me to type my misery. But I sat in stillness, music covering up any sounds of crying until the computer powered down, leaving no light at all.

I heard Jason move, the rattle of dog leads announcing his intentions. I quickly wiped away my tears so I could kiss him before he walked the dogs.

He opened the door.

"I'm just walking the dogs. I won't be long." He gave me a kiss and left me alone in the dark.

I hated that I was lying; lying with my body language, facial expressions and words. I hated that I wondered if he really didn't see, or he chose not to because he couldn't deal with it anymore. I hated everything that was me. I hated that this tale had become so repetitive. I wrote the same things again and again. I could find no new ways to express this blackness, it was all consuming. I wrote as I descended into depression. I wrote as I crawled my way back to the light. I wrote as I slipped and fell again. Over and over the story was repeated. I was learning that I would always slip and fall because I didn't have the strength to keep climbing; the walls were too steep and my muscles were shaking with fatigue. I was too weak and I hated myself for that too.

There was no one I felt I could share this with. Jason, Meredith, the people who supported me through the lowest ebbs were so happy to see me doing better. I had asked so much of them and it was unfair of me to keep asking. They needed a break, even if I didn't get one. They needed a chance to recharge before I assaulted them with my needs. I was trying so hard. I was trying to do things, to get chores done. But I was so tired at the end of the day, so tired from trying to be normal. So I hid in the darkness and hoped that Jason wouldn't open the door and see how bad it was.

Tonight I want to write the worst of me, berate myself with words. I want to hurt myself, force myself to confront my rotting heart. Tonight I want to punish myself. I deserve to suffer for my thoughts, for my selfishness. I deserve to suffer, because I am me. I want to stand on the rooftops and yell my deficits aloud, so that the rest of you will punish me; throw things at me, insult me, hate me. I want you to see the darkness inside, so that you will hate me too. How fucked is it to want to be hated?

The voice in my head says 'SUFFER'. It yells it at me, pushes my strength down and stops it with the force of the word. 'SUFFER' and soon it promises, soon I will yell 'DIE' and with only the strength of that word i know i will stop breathing. i did not ask for this. i do not want this. i am suffering. i give in. i will suffer until i am given permission to stop. The inner voice, my inner dialogue, racing thoughts that do not stop: you are weak. you are nothing. no one cares. you deserve this. you deserve it all. you deserve no happiness. there is no happiness for you. down, sink down into this darkness, do not try and fight because you cannot win. Down, I will push you down and you will stay until I let you up for air, if I choose to let you up for air.

i do not see the noose tonight, i see a razor blade cutting into my neck letting my blood flow freely. i hate this and this is me, so i hate me. i beg you to hate me too, see inside me and understand that i am broken and the good that was part of me has withered and died. i have lost this fight. i beg of you hate me. i am not worth love, it makes me feel like a fraud. If you think you love me, then you can't know me, because there is nothing in me worth loving.

A day later and those words disgusted me. I did not normally allow myself to dwell in my self-pity and voice the inner thoughts that plagued me, because to voice them gave them strength.

Temptation

28th September 2011.

Jason is away for a night, just one night. It is tempting, death is so tempting. No one would miss me until tomorrow. I can picture standing on the stool, the rope around my neck. Death is calling. I am rating my mood as mildly depressed, yet suicide is still here. The thoughts won't stop. They mull around my head. I don't like visualising my death all the time. Part of me just wants to hang the noose, put some weight on the rope. Not step off the stool, just get close to the edge. The difference with this more mild depression is that I know it would hurt people if I died. It is hard though, it is hard to live for them. Can you picture me now? Sitting in front of the computer, holding my head in my hands, my breath coming fast, shutting my eyes to get rid of the visions. My heart is racing and I feel agitated. I want so much to hang the noose again. This is the fight; this is the pointy end of the fight. If I hang the noose I may not stop. I know that. I have to halt it now, but fucking hell it's hard. If I get the rope, hold the rope I think that maybe it would help, maybe it would feel better. But what if I don't stop?

My breath is coming so fast.
If I don't stop, then I'm sorry.

145

I stopped

I tied the noose. I put it round my neck. I tightened it and felt the pressure on my skin. But I didn't tie it to anything. I stopped. This was such a private battle, fought in the dark, fought inside my head. I told no one what I did that night. I kept my battle private. I was so ashamed, so I told no one. Shame can kill. I kept telling everyone how well I was doing, that I was so much better. But I put a noose around my neck and pulled it tight. Shame kept me quiet. I did not want to disappoint. I wanted the medications to work, so I pretended they were. I was not just lying to everyone else, I was lying to myself. On my mood chart I rated my depression as mild, but can depression be mild when you put a noose around your neck and tighten it? I did not want to show it dropping, did not want that line to plummet again, so I lied to myself and pretended I was doing better.

***

Is anger better than sadness? A little thing sets me off and I yell, I scream, I bang doors and slam my hands into the wall over and over, trying to feel the pain. But when the anger fades I am stuck in the dark crying, with guilt and shame for company.

I watched a sad show with tears constantly streaming down my face. Jason commented that this was not the day for it. He didn't seem to understand the tears were for me, the show just made it socially acceptable. Watching something happy grated on me, reminded me of the things I could not feel, taunted me with joy whilst inside I was dying.

My thoughts continued to be consumed by death.

If I die in an accident or from some physical illness, will it be easier? I have written pages and pages of the why. I have said time and time again that it was no one's fault but mine. At this point does it really make a difference how I die? They would know, the people who care, that being dead would not have upset me even if I had no hand in my demise. I should stop this, I know, stop writing the dark thoughts. I should focus on the smell of a flower, the warmth of the sun, the uncomplicated love of my dogs. But they give me nothing. Scents are odourless. The sun doesn't penetrate deep enough to provide any warmth of all. The dogs just seem demanding, wanting more than I have to give.

I was struggling to cope. Although my safety was no longer at stake I found it so hard to cope with anything. I was completely out of strength. I stopped caring about anything, even whether I would go to hospital or not. One night I dropped a carving knife while making dinner and instinctively moved to catch it between my stomach and the table. I missed and it fell to the floor by my feet. I felt no relief that it hadn't cut me, no disappointment either. I just didn't care either way. I was numb.

The suicidal thoughts came easier now, with any little dip in mood. I think it was partly because they were memories, not just thoughts. I saw what I'd done, but from the outside. The colours were so bright. I saw myself standing on the white stool, the blue rope around my neck, the rich red sofa a contrasting background. I would see my knees bend as I put weight on the rope and it bit into my skin limiting the blood to my brain. I remembered it, I felt it, everything was in such sharp relief. I just wanted it to stop.

One of the worst aspects of this more mildly depressed state was the lack of pleasure, lack of enthusiasm, lack of excitement. I was going to take Meredith to see 'Mary Poppins' for her birthday and I love musicals. Everyone I'd spoken to absolutely loved it. Yet I couldn't manage to muster any enthusiasm. I felt like I should be excitedly telling everyone that I was going, but that would have been so unbelievably fake because all I could think was that it was an awful lot of effort and another late night. It was the same with travel. I heard about other people's travel plans and although I knew that they were places I wanted to go; places that are fascinating and interesting, the idea of going myself held no appeal. All I could see was the immense effort that would be involved. Not just the effort involved in planning, but also the effort involved in actually seeing the sights, travelling and having to pretend to enjoy myself.

Part of me wondered why I kept trying, what the point was in expending so much effort to keep going to work and doing activities that should be fun. I was so exhausted. I think it is difficult to convey in words how unbelievably tiring it was. I get why so many depressed people do stop trying. It was like carrying 20kg on my back everywhere I went, whilst people followed me around whipping me to cause me pain and the ground was a foot deep in mud. There was no chance to rest, no opportunity to sit down and gather my energy to keep going. Yet I kept pushing through. I just wanted to lie down, rest and recharge. The real sting was that I knew if I took a week off work, I would just sink into myself, become consumed by the blackness and take no enjoyment in having time off. So I had to keep going until... until...

That's where I got stuck, because I couldn't see the light at the end of the tunnel. I didn't know if I would get a chance to rest.

The morning I was going to see 'Mary Poppins' I sat in my office with my hands around my neck and squeezed them tight. I felt my pulse fighting the pressure of my hands. It was a fragile thing beating against me and it would have been so easy to press a little harder and block its way. It was the pressure on the underside of my jaw that felt so uncomfortable when my weight was on the rope. So I pushed my hands up there and tried to desensitise myself to the unpleasantness of it. Exposure therapy. I don't think anyone would have approved of it.

Part Five

Healing

Can I skip this bit?

As my mood lifted I was desperate to reach recovery and return to my old self. I wanted to skip the healing needed and reach the finish line. After three days without tears I was questioning how I could 'get over it'.

It seemed like everyone else had just moved on. They were worried for so long, but once the crisis had passed and my life was not at stake, they were able to move on with their lives. They went back to worrying about the small things, taking pleasure where they could and being who they'd always been. I couldn't do that. I was not who I always was. The preceding twelve months had changed everything. My world had been turned upside down and yet on the outside it appeared just the same. I had to accept that I have bipolar disorder and that I can't necessarily control that part of me. I had to come to terms with the fact that I am a person who could kill myself. I may have got close to the edge many times in my life, but now I know that at some point I could cross the line. Maybe there will come a time when I descend back into the darkness and don't survive to tell about it.

***

"Jason. Can we talk?"

He stopped cooking and came to sit with me at the dining table. I sat and fiddled with my empty glass, turning it around in my hands, running my fingers up and down the outside. Jason sat patiently waiting, giving me time to collect my thoughts.

"It's..." I cleared my throat, my mouth had become dry and my tongue stuck to the roof of my mouth. "I wouldn't have killed myself if I'd been put in hospital." My heart sped up in my chest, my blood pumping audibly in my ears. "If it happens again, you should tell my psychiatrist what's going on. You need to let her know if I'm not safe. If you need to, you should put me in hospital."

It was tremendously difficult to say those words. Not because I wanted to die rather than face the consequences of being in hospital, but because I remembered the agony, the pain and the horrendous struggle to breathe. The idea of having to go through that again terrified me and part of me believed that if it came back now I was on medication then it would just keep coming back. I didn't think I had the strength to survive that again. But at the same time, I was glad that I wasn't dead. I was glad that I had not been the cause of pain and suffering to those I love. So whilst in my rational mind I needed to make the difficult decisions.

I searched for information on how to recover from a suicide attempt, but what I found was trite suggestions that talked about seeing your friends again and doing activities you enjoy. But that doesn't address the underlying issue. That doesn't actually fix anything. I did those things. I did not check out of life, quit my job and alienate my friends. But my emotional state was still fragile and I wanted help finding my way.

What line should I be walking with these thoughts I have? I know it is not good to dwell in the memories, to focus on that suicidal part of me, but at the same time if I try to not think of them then it will only make them stronger and give them more weight. So there must be a line somewhere between avoidance and dwelling that I need to find. I wonder if it is different when you have taken an overdose, rather than engaged in a more violent method. I guess I can't know that. But I would think that memories of taking pills (normal activity), feeling ill (part of life), being in hospital (not altogether a new experience) would not hold the same salience that memories of tying a noose around your neck, jumping off a stool and feeling your whole body weight suspended by your neck have. Those memories can in no way be minimised to dismiss the suicidal intent behind them.

There was nothing I found that talked about how you deal with reminders. Every little thing reminded me. I stepped out the back door and saw the beam that was going to be the last thing I ever saw and was reminded. I sat in the living room and was reminded. Every time I caught a glimpse of the rich red of the sofa I was reminded.

Then there were the bigger things like a client who hung himself, albeit accidentally. I had to read through the medical record that described in excruciating detail how it happened, how he was found. My head translated the words into a picture. The picture wouldn't shift and I felt my mood deteriorating and questioning if he could be unconscious too quickly to save himself, why couldn't I.

Jason and I took it slowly. Relapse was still feared, stability felt a breath away from dissolving. We decided to keep things calm and avoid anything that could cause an unexpected gust. We spoke quite specifically about traveling. We decided that until I had been stable for six months we would make no plans to travel overseas. The risk of depression in a foreign land felt too great.

For me part of moving forward involved telling friends, in particular Jenny and Mark. They were some of my closest friends and I was so aware when I was with them that they didn't know. I think if I hadn't told them what had happened, that I would have found myself retreating from them, as it had changed me from who they got to know.

This was one of the most difficult conversations I could think of and I had no idea where to start. I had no idea which words to use. I didn't know how to bring up the topic of suicide. When I was telling Jenny about having bipolar and being depressed I saw her panic when I mentioned the 'ledge incident' and her relief when I told her it was a hallucination. I decided then and there not to tell her about the real ledge incidents, the ones where I had stood on the edge of the cliff and had to be the one to talk myself out of jumping. But it was different now. They nearly found out in the worst possible way, so I needed to let them know more gently.

Words that ran through my head, flippant words which were totally inappropriate.

I was nearly an involuntary psychiatric inpatient.

I only tried to kill myself once this year.

I'm still here but only because we have low ceilings and dodgy ropes.

What I hoped to do was explain what depression is for me. That it is not about reality. To explain the total loss of pleasure, the hopelessness and the irrational thoughts that take root and can't be shifted despite knowing in some part of me that they are irrational, delusional even. I had a feeling though that when it came down to it I would not find the words I wanted to say. What came out of my mouth would be stilted, said softly, vaguely whilst I willed them to understand what I was trying to say.

How <u>not</u> to tell someone you tried to kill yourself - version 3

I wouldn't be able to do this in a normal conversation. I had to make sure I couldn't back out. I sent a text, so that she would prompt me to do the telling.

Can I come over? There's something I need to tell you.

Seconds later my phone rang.
"Are you ok? What do you need to tell me?"
"I want to tell you face to face."
"You're scaring me."

The next day I walked up the flight of stairs to their flat and was greeted at the door by Jenny and Mark, given warm, welcoming hugs. I had never before seen their apartment in chaos, it is usually impeccably clean, but they were the middle of renovating and not expecting visitors. Mark moved away to the other room, busying himself to give Jenny and I some privacy. We sat down beside each other on their new green sofa.
     "I love this colour." I still didn't know how to shift this conversation to where it needed to go, but Jenny did it for me.

ELLEN NORTHCOTT

"What do you need to tell me?" She looked at me, her worried eyes and brisk voice. We needed to do it quickly, like a bandaid.

I turned my head away from her, looking for the words. My eyes focussed on a plant on the windowsill as if it would have the answers. I found myself crying and all my gentle introductions to the topic failed. I looked back to her with tears now streaming down my face.

"I tried to kill myself."

How <u>not</u> to tell someone you tried to kill yourself - version 4

I thought initially that with other friends it wouldn't matter, that I would be able to talk about unimportant things without my secrets being on the tip of my tongue. But I found in every situation, with any-one who knew me well that it was there caught in the back of my throat; the desire to just let it out and shock with my words.

I had a dinner coming up with a group of long time friends who get together all too rarely. It was not the place to raise depression or suicide, but it was too big a part of my thoughts to be kept a secret. So I sent an email, apologetic for my painful words.

I am lucky in the friends that I have, that noth-ing changed. Each person was different, some people had questions, some had their own stories to share with me. Some people found the discussion uncomfortable, not sure what to say or do with depression. But with each friend that I chose to tell, I was reassured that I am loved. No one pulled away or treated me like I have some horrible contagion. If I was changed in their eyes it was not apparent to me.

The power of words

There are many words that are used to describe people with mental illness which are considered politically incorrect and stigmatising. Crazy, nuts or insane to name a few. These terms have never bothered me. I was called them before I knew I had a mental illness, so I see no reason to take offence now that I know I have one. Admittedly these words have only been applied to me with fun, in jest or with love. I have not had them thrown in my face designed to wound. If I had, I'm sure my feelings would be different.

The term that I struggle most with is psychotic. I'll admit to being crazy, but I squirm at having to admit to psychotic symptoms. Each time I saw a new doctor, or psychologist, and they went through their list of questions I always gave an emphatic 'No' when it came to things that may be classed psychotic. Hallucinations? No! Delusions? No!

It wasn't that I was lying, but I was still maintaining what denial I could. I had given up my notion of normalcy, but to admit to the complete disconnect with reality that psychosis suggests was still beyond me. I didn't consider the elves psychotic, it was the two people I discussed them with, Jason and Meredith, who did that. The constant visions of being stabbed in the neck, were not something I classed as hallucinations. I just had an overactive imagination. That I deserved to die was not a delusion, it was a fact. The earlier delusions, paranoia, magic powers, were amusing anecdotes and not a reflection of psychosis.

Words have a great deal of power, and each person has particular words that when assigned become a burdensome label. Mental illness. Depression. Bipolar disorder. Manic. Crazy. Insane. Psychotic. It will take some time to convince myself it's just another word, that describes some experiences I've had which are a little outside the norm. It doesn't make me less. It doesn't change me. Psychotic.

Inspiration

"Are you manic?"

I bounced around the house so high on life. I
called friend after friend wanting to talk to someone, to
share the excitement and my joy with life. I watched
Frozen Planet, a documentary about Antarctica, and less
than 24 hours later I had booked a trip to Antarctica
leaving in six weeks. I maxed out the credit cards, emptied our bank account, emptied my savings account,
emptied Jason's savings account and still came up short
of what I needed.

"You're sounding awfully manic."

No, not manic. It had just been so long feeling
depressed that no one remembered what I was like before, not even me. Words stumbled out of my mouth as
I talked and talked about travel, about work, about this
and that and nothing in-between. I could feel that my
speech was fast, faster than normal but it was just because there was so much to say. My friends teased me
for moving around so much, for being unable to be still,
even for a minute. Even at work I was unable to sit
completely still, my energy transferring to the constant
twitching of my legs. I caught people looking at my
ever moving legs, but it took such an effort of will to
stay still that I couldn't do that and concentrate on work
at the same time. I found myself wearing clothes I

hadn't worn for months. The clothes that were tight, the necklines lower and I felt good. I knew I hadn't lost weight, but I just looked better than I did. I felt sexy and confident within myself.

"You're manic."

Maybe I conceded, maybe I was verging on the edge of hypomania, but not manic. This felt so good. I was not thinking about any of the darkness I had been through, it seemed like it happened to someone else and had no bearing on this new world of light and joy.

My acting classes evolved, inspired me. The school ran a year long all time course, for aspiring actors. This would be my new career! I would quit psychology, return to acting but take it seriously this time. It was a few thousand dollars and a year of unemployment. But I was brilliant, it would pay for itself once I was famous!

Stumble

The path out isn't easy. I had a few good weeks and I forgot. I felt a little stronger. I was so aware that the rope was still there. Hidden away, but there like a shining beacon. It was time for it to go.

I knew it would be hard, which is why I hadn't touched it yet. But I also thought with my joy, with the promise of new discoveries that I would be protected. So I wasn't prepared for it to break me. I wasn't prepared to find myself sobbing, trembling, assaulted with emotions I couldn't label. Although it was not the rope I used for the actual suicide attempt, it was the rope I purchased specifically to bring my own death. When the visions came they were of the times I had that rope around my neck, placed my weight on it but didn't step off the stool. I don't know why they were more salient. I felt the other should have been, but it was that second rope that haunted me. I don't know how to explain this, because I did not expect such a little thing to break through my defences and bring me to my knees.

Another day, another event knocked me over. The report for that boy who accidentally hung himself still needed to be written. I spent ten minutes looking through his medical records and on every page the words jumped out at me "HANGING", "STRANGULA-

TION" flashing red on every page no matter how small the actual font. Each word, each page of the medical record and I saw myself hanging, felt the rope around my neck, my head bent back and the blue sky fading to blackness. I saw myself die with each word. I had to leave and go outside to sit and cry for thirty minutes. I didn't know how I would write this report, how I would spend enough time on his medical record to get it done. Part of me wanted to admit defeat, ask for help to get someone else to read the file, but there was that other part that needed to prove to myself that I was strong enough for this.

The moment I'd been putting off had come. It was time for me to tell my boss and those I worked most closely with.

How <u>not</u> to tell someone you tried to kill yourself - version 5

I paced the corridor, rehearsing my speech in my head. Why I felt a need to tell him, that I didn't want it to change anything. Justifying myself as to why I couldn't keep this secret. I would follow the why with a diagnosis, simple words with a myriad of possible meanings.

I knocked on the door.

"Come in." I shut the door behind me, a closed door conversation a departure from the norm. "What can I do for you?"

My voice was trembling, my palms sweating, my eyes anywhere but his. A quick glance and my rehearsed speech was lost. The justification sounded wrong as it left my lips. The hard bit now, the part that will shock, that awful word suicide. Then I stopped. My mouth was dry, the words had become stuck on their way out.

"I had no idea." Of course he didn't. If he had then surely he would have done something, said something. He wouldn't have seen me every day and thought me suicidal without feeling some responsibility to ask if I was ok. I assume, at least, that he would not have done that. But I knew that he said such a banal statement, because there was nothing else to say. It was a way to fill the silence whilst he coped with his shock.

Then he asked what it was I wanted from this telling. Did I want to be monitored? Did I want to have someone check up on me? It was so hard to explain that all I wanted was not to feel like I was keeping some horrible secret. There was really no other reason for me to tell him.

How <u>not</u> to tell someone you tried to kill yourself - version 6

It was another day and it came back in full flight. Flashback.

I was sitting in my office, but I was back standing on a stool with the noose tightening around my neck. My breath came in short ragged bursts and tears welled in my eyes. I needed someone to sit with me, keep my grounded. I asked if I could come into her office. I hadn't spoken to her yet, so this was probably unfair.

"Are you ok?"

"No." She looked at me expecting more, confused and bewildered as I broke down before her eyes. It came out all wrong. In my state of blind panic I forgot the niceties, I forgot she had no idea that I was anything other than sane.

"I can't breathe, I hung myself and I can't breathe." She sat in shock. Where do we go from here? This conversation was too filled with panic from both our sides for any real understanding to be given.

"Do you want some chocolate?" Her suggested solution, to an unsolvable problem.

Part Six

Relapse

A little niggle

What happens when that magic medicine, the one that dragged you back from the brink stops working? What happens then?

I naively thought I would finish there. A year of writing. A catalyst year that moved from denial, tentative acceptance, ecstasy, despair and suicide to some trembling stability. Why I thought that one year would cover it all, would encapsulate the entirety of my struggle with mental illness, I'm not sure. I didn't think I was heading for a happily ever after, but I did think I had said what needed to be said. I did, perhaps, assume that my moods would remain broadly within the scope of normal. Despite being aware of the literature that suggests up to 80% of people will have a mood relapse within five years, I believed that I would be in that 20% so long as I remained medication compliant. It therefore seemed to follow that I would have nothing more to write, that a life without moods would be boring and ordinary. But life does not end, irrespective of my state of mind.

2012 started brilliantly. We welcomed the New Year at the official end of the world, the most southern point of Argentina. From there we travelled south for an amazing two weeks cruising alongside the Antartican peninsular. For a holiday booked in feverish mania it seemed doubtful that it would be worth the extortionate price. After an unexpectedly calm trip across the Drake Passage we caught sight of our first iceberg, a brilliant blue brush stroke in otherwise grey scenery. We were soon surrounded by icebergs of many shapes and sizes. We learnt the difference between icebergs, bergy bits and growlers. Ice came as sea ice, black ice, pancake ice and brash ice. Icebergs came dotted by airpockets, striped as if by a massive paintbrush, beautiful curves and towering cliffs. Glaciers carved their way down mountains, beautifully blue or lined with black soil dredged up from below. Penguin colonies announced themselves with a pungent odour and unmistakable penguin squawks. After the first full day in Antarctica proper it became clear that this trip was worth every penny we had spent. Around the dinner table that night every other passenger articulated the same thought. It seemed even if we saw nothing else we had received our monies worth. Of course the highlights were by no means over, with close encounters with humpback whales, weddel and elephant seals as well as thousands of penguins still to come.

One night as we were about to eat dinner there was an announcement to say that a whale was breaching on the starboard side of the boat. Despite sitting on the furthest side of the dining room from the door I was the second person out, sprinting up the stairs to the outside. Over and over the whale launched himself out of the water, crashing back down to the "Ahhhs" of nearly one hundred witnesses. Once I could take the cold no longer I rushed inside to get my jacket, aware of each breach by the cries of joy that echoed through the ship. I stayed to the last, each passenger succumbing to cold or hunger until only a handful remained. Eventually the captain announced we were moving on, leaving the whale to continue his play alone. As I sat at dinner that night I was teased for the extent of my smile, that all overwhelming joy that shone on my face. A natural high that owed nothing to mood disorders.

On our last day as we sat at dinner once more, the only thing we had not been lucky enough to see was orcas. Jokingly our guide telephoned the bridge to relay our request. Not five minutes later they called back to say there were orcas just off the port side of the ship. Again I held no regard for the temperature running out onto the deck in only a t-shirt, where I stood astounded as we were surrounded by a pod of around forty orcas. Cuddling up to a stranger who had also not bothered to get a jacket for warmth I stood transfixed. There are no words that can truly relate the Antarctica experience, and no photo truly captures the beauty. It is this, more than anything, that makes the journey so special, as it is not something you have seen before.

Returning home from such an adventure was difficult, but life continued to rumble along for the next five months. We kept things simple, made no momentous plans. We gradually started to pay off the debts incurred through mania. Any further renovation to the house was put on hold and any potential stressor was to be avoided. Stability was to be enjoyed and kept in our tentative grasp.

But my grip started to slip.

At first it was a little niggle, not much, just a loss of interest, a bit of sadness and a reluctance to do anything. It seemed no more than anyone might feel in a down period, no real cause for concern, just something to watch. I saw friends and perked up, felt real laughter. But then the niggle returned, a little deeper now and a little more serious. But still I felt I could smile at times, laugh at times. I had another dinner coming up, more friends to help me rally to keep smiling. And smile I did, not just at dinner, but the next day when my friend had a baby. Just like that I felt normal, I felt so excited for her when I went to hold that new life. But the next day I crashed, lower now, not a niggle anymore.

I added the anti-psychotic back into my medication regime, the back up plan discussed with my psychiatrist for if things slid backwards. I looked to yet another night out with friends hoping beyond hope that it would keep me going, help me back to stable. As I reached the restaurant I turned away, sat out of sight crying, unsure if I should go in, unsure if I could stop the tears, unsure if they would even want me there. I tried entering the restaurant plastering a smile on my face, but I felt like such an intruder. I was a black swirling vortex, unable to absorb even a part of their happiness. Just a chain dragging them down with me.

It was terrifying this uncertainty, this knowledge that I am not one of the lucky ones who can stay stable as long as I keep taking my medication. On the Monday I went to work, keeping up the image of normality. But my mask was destroyed. I was open, raw, exposed. Once the first tear fell, they didn't stop. I left work, walking all the way home whilst my tears marked the trail. For five hours I wept my pain, my fear, my despair. Anger and depression, fear and sadness all of which I put on Facebook. My pain, my shame for all the world to see. I had seen the outcome when I didn't talk, so from one extreme to the other, I started yelling so that the ending would be different. My friends responded, they called, they texted, they messaged me on Facebook. My friends showed that they cared, said they were there if I needed to talk. It made such a difference, but there was still a lack of understanding.

They said they were sorry that I was having a tough time, rough time, that I seemed bummed. It was not tough or rough. I was not bummed. The first thing I saw when I woke up in the morning was my hand ripping my heart out of my chest. The scalpel cutting my skin and my flesh falling away like wrapping paper. My ribs easily broken by the pressure of my hand reaching down. Insubstantial, hardly there at all. This was fear, distress, uncertainty. I knew they said the words with caring, but the words emphasised their lack of understanding.

The best thing they did, the thing that made the biggest difference was coming to spend time with me. I don't mean coming to check on me or have big deep and meaningful conversation, but just doing the things we would normally do together. It helped to be reminded that I had friends who wanted to spend time with me.

For the first time I took time off work for my depression, prioritising getting a doctor's appointment over my job. I saw my psychiatrist, so we could try this medication, increase the dose of that one. We talked about the other options, each different chemical that may work better or differently at least. I complied meekly, nodding my agreement even as my belief that this would get better faded. The following day I was off work, but I had no plans, and I sat still, unmoving. I achieved nothing all day, did nothing and did not care that I had hardly moved. Taking time off work was not beneficial for me. Going to work was impossibly hard, but at least it kept me from turning into a statue.

Insanity was calling, beckoning me away from safety. I wanted to go. I wanted to step out onto that narrow beam whilst Jason called me back.

I fall to my knees, looking out. Sit on the edge and look down to see the black below. Raging and calling me, still as the darkest night. I want to feel. I find myself over and over again wanting to stop taking my medication. It gives me freedom, but takes my feelings. I miss out on the extremes, so I miss all of me and I wonder if that's living at all. If my moods are part of me and they change me, shape me into a new person then controlling them is cutting short who I could be. I think it is hard for others to see why I would even consider stopping the medication, particularly now when things are heading down. I feel that if I don't reach the bottom, then I won't come back. I am terrified and curious of where I would go. I want to, but in the same breath, the same thought I desperately don't want to. There is no middle ground and I am frustrated resting in this place between true depression and stability. I like the extremes. I'm an all or nothing kind of girl. So take me and lift me up as high as possible before dropping me and watch as I break into a million pieces. Take me, fill me with pain, fill me with desire, show me everything the world has to offer and don't doubt that that includes pain as well as joy. Then forgive me that I choose to sabotage myself. Forgive me that I choose to take a risk, for I know I risk your heart as well as my own.

Break me. I dare you. I beg you. Break me.

I should change my thinking, look for the positive in everything. Look for the positive in me, not see the dark twisted part that revels in despair. Gradually I sink a little more, believe a little more that this is my just desserts. Perhaps I was right all along believing that suffering is what I deserve.

But what ye wish shall come to pass. The pain came sharp and immediate, as deadly as any knife. The sharp decline to the place that breathing hurts and death seems a welcome release. I realised the folly of thinking this could ever be a choice I would make.

The secret

My medications were changing, experimenting with my mind to try and clear away the blackness. From one day to the next the world changed from the deepest black to a startling kaleidoscope of colours shifting in an ever more beautiful pattern.

I felt like I knew a secret that the rest of the world was missing, and that secret spread over my face until my cheeks hurt from smiling.

I stepped out the door and for a moment I paused, suspended in mid-motion, awed by the beauty that I saw. The beautiful blue sky, the warmth of the sun on my face, the clouds floating behind the trees, the dark underside of storm clouds, the feel of cold air on my face as stars twinkled about me, the most perfect crescent moon, the detailed full moon, the wind moving through me and around me. Every time I stepped out the door I was struck anew at the beauty of the world, no matter what it was I saw. This, for me, is part of what it means to be manic, hypomanic, high, on top of the world. Whatever you call it, this is what I live for.

I moved from my state of suspended animation and the world started turning again, and I didn't stop. I danced down the street, because walking was too slow and sedentary. I would be at home, but still I didn't, couldn't, wouldn't stop.

I took ideas that flowed incessantly through my mind, caught hold of one of many and took it for a ride. Travel took over and I planned holidays, bought hundreds of dollars' worth of guidebooks, booked tours and flights with no consideration of the cost.

I decided to start a photography business. Within two hours I had filled in all the necessary documentation on line and was officially a registered business. I was convinced that with just a little effort my photography skills would become world renowned, and I would be able to fund my travel habit through selling photos to an ever appreciative audience. I entered a photo into an international photography competition. Just one photo, in one competition but I knew that this would start my meteoric rise to fame.

I met up with Meredith to do some shopping. I was shooting a wedding on the weekend, and my black trousers were falling off me. I had dropped a dress size in 3 weeks. We went into shops I would normally dismiss as too expensive. My interest in clothes being minimal, my budget didn't normally stretch that far. We quickly found some trousers that fitted and were heading towards the check out.

I pointed out a beautiful dress. "Isn't that gorgeous?"

"Why don't you try it on?"

"When have you ever seen me in a dress?"

Meredith paused. "Surely I have." I gave her time to think. "No, I haven't. Come on try it on."

I tried on dress after dress. There was one particular dress, a startling green and black one, that I kept going back to.

"It's perfect on you."

"But when would I ever wear it?" I couldn't help but look in the mirror again. It really did look good.

"You can use it as an excuse to go out."

I looked at the price tag. "This is ridiculous! That's my normal clothes budget for a year."

"It looks great though."

I succumbed to the moment. "Alright then!"

All of a sudden Meredith looked worried. "You don't have to. I don't want you to do something you'll regret. Am I encouraging your mania?"

"Don't be silly." I gave her a cheeky grin. "But, I'll need shoes to wear with it!"

I was completed seduced with feeling pretty and wanted more. I used my shrinking frame as a rationalisation for restocking my wardrobe. I purchased dresses, shoes, jackets. When I headed into work the next week I relished the reactions.

"Wow! Do you have a date or something?"

"Look at you. Very pretty."

"Do you have an interview?"

"This is new."

"Very fancy."

***

It had been a month since I last saw my psychiatrist, I had been depressed last time she saw me.

She held the door to her office open for me. "How are things?"

"Good." I said with a smile.

"Really?" She checked, knowing my habit of minimising when things were bad.

"Yes, really. I feel good."

"That's great." She said with a smile. Then she paused and looked at me, registering my obvious joy that was not normally present at these appointments. "Good, or very good?"

"Maybe a little bit very good." My grin expanded despite my best efforts to control it.

"Hmmm. Tell me what's been happening." Her face became more serious again.

There had been so much that had gone on in the last month that I was not sure where to start. I picked on the big things. The trips I'd purchased. I'd painted the living room. My photography business.

"What sort of photography business?"

"Well. I haven't really decided. I was going to make it for weddings and portraits, but I'm not sure. I would rather do fine art photography, I think. I don't know. I keep redoing my website. I'm shooting a wedding this weekend." The words were rushing out too fast, so I closed my mouth trying not to give myself away.

She gave me a knowing smile and jotted something down in her notes.

She motioned to my legs. "Do they always move like that?"

I hadn't been aware they were moving. I was doing my best to stay still.

"No, not normally." I tried to stop them, but only kept them still for mere seconds. She'd seen me often enough that she didn't really need my answer. She just wanted to point it out to me.

She wanted to bring me down, use medication to return me to stability. But in my mind this was not a condition that required treatment, it did not need fixing. Though I saw that my behaviour was not quite what it was, I could see no reason it needed to be changed. I had been paid in full for the preceding six weeks of depression, and didn't want it to end. She told me to increase the amount of the anti-psychotic, Seroquel, I was taking. She tried to explain why I needed to modify this mood.

"How's your irritability? Are you getting into fights?"

"No, I'm not getting into fights. A bit irritable, but not too much." Jason would have disagreed with my summation. He bared the brunt of my irritable moments, but they hardly registered with me.

"Your judgement is impaired." No, I wanted to tell her, it's inspired. She continued. "It's exhausting for those around you." But I knew it wasn't. They loved being with me to catch the edge of this euphoria.

I didn't present my arguments, I knew I could not convince her of my sanity, and she could not convince me otherwise.

Then I started to get sick, my body running itself into the ground from constant activity and lack of sleep. Jason had to force me to eat, placing a bowl of food in my hand as I danced around the house. I was unable to sit at the table. I had too much stored energy from sitting still at work. As soon as I increased the Seroquel as directed, sleep returned, and I quickly felt healthier. The dose was not enough to end the high and return my rational brain. It was just enough to slow me down and give sleep a chance to overwhelm me. After two nights with a reasonable amount of rest I would feel healthier again and chase the high by reducing the Seroquel once more. I continued this pattern increasing the Seroquel repeatedly only long enough for my body to recover. The high continued, escalated, tipped from hypomania to mania.

I raced down the street at 1am, letting the dogs pull me forward as I struggled to breathe for laughter.

In a brief moment of insight I realised that I was now the crazy lady in the neighbourhood, which only made me laugh harder.

In a stroke of genius I saw how much better the house would look with one less wall. We were eating dinner when the thought occurred to me and I jumped from my seat with excitement. Our entrance way was so small and closed in that I decided we should remove the wall between it and the kitchen. Jason listened to my feverish excitement, but shook his head "No."

I was not used to this reaction. My excitement is contagious and I could normally bring Jason along, giving him some of my enthusiasm. I continued to expound upon the benefits of my idea, even drew an outline of where the new opening would be. It was not just the advisability of knocking down a potentially structural wall, or the difficulties in fixing up the mess afterwards that he was against. Jason did not think it would look good, so he was firm.

It was with a giggle and a covert look that I picked up the hammer and made that first hole. Jason took the hammer, reiterated that he didn't want this to happen. Then he went to bed. He had stopped trying to keep up with me at this point. I was sleeping so little and doing so much. Whilst he slept I gradually widened the hole.

By morning the wall was gone. I was so pleased with myself, sure that Jason would be convinced of the brilliance of my idea.

"Was it structural?" It was always the first question when I told people what I'd done the night before. I was so convinced it wasn't structural, certain I was too knowledgeable to make such a blatant error. But others continued to question how I knew that, with my non-existent engineering and building knowledge. At the time I was certain I knew everything.

I continued my nightly activities, Jason slightly worried now as to what he would find in the morning. Sleep had become an optional extra. I was constantly full of energy, enthusiasm and plans. There was inspiration in every sentence, and wherever I looked ideas flowed as to what could be done. The bank account ran down to empty as the fruits of my enthusiasm arrived at my door.

An email arrived in my inbox offering four pole dancing lessons for $39. Why not? I signed up, not sure what I was getting myself into.

I took back my role of saviour, determined to make a difference to the world. Although I was able to afford the cost of lamotrigine, it was not approved by the PBS for the treatment of bipolar disorder and was therefore out of reach of the people who need it most. I started to collect journal articles and financial reports, preparing my presentation for the government.

All the while I danced, ran, laughed with unadulterated joy. I danced on picnic tables in the park. I danced unashamedly in the sun in my lunch break. I danced in front of our uncurtained windows for all the world to see.

My thoughts didn't always connect, distracted by each intervening image, sight and sound. But everything was so clear to me. Because I knew the secret that the rest of the world just wish they knew and the smile spread over my face once more.

Fighting calm

Despite an ever increasing list of activities when I next saw my psychiatrist I didn't make it past the wall. Once I had told her of my impromptu renovation her faced mimicked those who I had told at work.

"Was it structural?"

"No. The roof is still standing." I said with a laugh. The whole thing was so hilarious.

"We really need to bring you down. I want you to increase the Seroquel some more. Do you think it would sedate you if you took a small dose during the day?"

"No, I don't imagine it would." I said with a chuckle. The night time dose was barely enough to sedate me, a small dose was unlikely to register at all.

"I want you to take 50mg in the afternoon to try and calm you down in addition to increasing the night time dose."

I was really not keen and it showed on my face.

"It's either that or I can prescribe you Diazepam. But you need to take something. If you can't calm yourself down, we need to do it chemically. This can't continue. Which would you prefer?"

"Fine. I'll stick with the Seroquel."

"That's what I thought. Now, do you have enough Seroquel, or do I need to write you another prescription?"

Two months into the mania I felt that it was worth the worst 2011 had to offer, it was worth the risk of death by suicide. It is a seductive drug, mania, one that in the moment is worth dying for. I was told repeatedly I needed to bring myself down with medication so that I did not crash and burn into another depression. But that argument holds little weight when you are flying through the clouds and hell belongs to another.

My mania is not all sunlight and flowers though, that would be misleading.

I pace up and down screaming at my head to stop. Nothing is fast enough, all music is so slow it is infuriating. Pacing, pacing, pacing. I want to hit, to scream, to tear the world to shreds. Pounding thoughts, nothing coherent. Just frustration, irritability, anger at a world that won't keep up. I bite my hand, clamp down to muffle the screams and keep me grounded so I don't throw everything I own away, through windows just to hear the shattering sound.

"SHUT UP! SHUT THE FUCK UP!"

Jason comes running from the other end of the house. "What's wrong? I heard you yelling."

"It just won't shut up." I can't think, because there are too many thoughts and they are too loud.

There is a charming medical term called insight, the ability to see yourself clearly, be aware of your behaviour, emotions and symptoms. Mania is characterised by decreased insight, so the higher the flight, the less problematic it seems. Imagine that you feel great. You are productive, amazingly happy with little reason, problems pale into insignificance and you have energy to spare. In this state your feet are still firmly on the ground and there are more positives than negatives, and you retain enough insight to know that this feeling of well-being is artificial. But as hypomania shifts into mania you stop needing sleep. You fly higher and faster. You are all capable and money seems to come from a limitless supply. You lie on the floor laughing because you don't know how to stop. People stare at your bizarre behaviour and you accept the attention as your due, they see how amazing you are too. As your feet lost contact with the ground, you forgot that that's where they were supposed to be. As mania gains more negatives than positives you lose sight of either. When my husband pointed out my outlandish behaviour, my deleterious mania, I laughed back hysterically, not believing a word he said. Insight had faded into the night as I danced under the midday sun.

Meredith comes over to meet me for swimming one evening, but I am rolling on the floor laughing. The dog had licked my face, or I had thought a funny thought I don't remember. I tried to get up to say hello, but laughter convulsed my body until I couldn't stand. Jason is used to this behaviour, but Meredith stands there, unsure what to do. I am too far gone for a rational conversation and I think I am hilarious. For 20 minutes she talks to Jason, whilst they ignore the laughing hysterical mess on the floor. We eventually make it to the pool, but every so often I succumb to laughter, falling beneath the water to muffle the sound.

I was keeping a mood chart for my psychiatrist, and each day Jason and I would discuss what number to assign, zero being baseline and five the highest I've ever been. Occasionally we would agree, but more often he would suggest my mood was much more elevated that I was willing to admit. For one week we kept individual records, with no discussion of where we believed my mood to be. For that week I consistently rated my mood at one, an acknowledgement that my mood was elevated but that was all. His ratings hovered between four and five and I dismissed them as nonsensical.

It is a night like any other. I am in the kitchen making dinner. I talk, I laugh, I dance as I chop vegetables and twirl through the chaos in my mind. I find myself holding two carving knives getting the balance of them, ready to juggle them when a breath of sanity whispers in my ear. I put the knives down and reach for the medicine cabinet, sedating myself to safety.

As I finally took the medication as prescribed a sense of calmness ensued and I relished it. It was a happiness that comes with peace and stillness. It was not the artificial euphoria that mania provides, but all the more valuable because of it.

Aftereffects

I was lucky to land safely, a gentle descent back
to earth. After such a lengthy time so far aloft there
were bound to be ramifications. I was firmly ensconced
as 'crazy' at work by all and sundry, each day asked what
new adventure had occurred the day before. My cloth-
ing had changed dramatically and I had lost fifteen kilo-
grams. I was rock climbing two or three times a week
and had taken up pole dancing in my manic frenzy. I
had a photography business, with no plan on how to
progress beyond a website and a business card. There
was a wall missing from the kitchen, which luckily had
not been structural. The living room had changed
colour and there were maps plastered on the wall with
lines depicting possible year long adventures.

Travel is my weakness, and without control of
my impulses holidays become excessive. Clare, who
lived in Berlin, was getting married and we always
knew we would go to her wedding. But with the excess
of manic plans what should have been a three week va-
cation was now a nine week adventure through Europe
and the Middle East. Our bank account was empty and
our mortgage higher as we had had to take money out
to cover my purchases.

But perhaps the greatest change was within me.
I felt healed; the mania had blasted away the remaining

cobwebs, a consequence in part due to a greater acceptance of my diagnosis. I tend to think I am making up
the highs, exaggerating a generally happy mood. But I
finally had some objective evidence.

One of the neuropsychological tests I routinely
administer is a computer based task that assesses attention and impulsivity. Towards the end of the mania I
completed this task and found to my intense amusement
that I couldn't do it. Of course at that time everything
was amusing. I was unable to inhibit my automatic response no matter how hard I tried. I tried to slow down
to give myself time to restrain my impulses. At the end
the computer told me that although I had no problems
with attention my impulsivity was off the charts. My
responses were atypically fast with a large number of
errors. What's more, despite my conscious effort to
slow myself down there was no change in my reaction
times across the fifteen minute test. This alone was not
enough to convince me. After all it may just have been
that I have an impulsive personality, or that this task is
in some way flawed. It was a few weeks later with my
feet firmly back on the ground when I again attempted
this task that I became convinced. It was easy, ridicu-
lously so, and the computer found no issues with either
attention or impulse control. The only conclusion was
that I really did have neurologically based problems
with impulse control, because despite excellent effort I
was unable to inhibit my responses when manic.

I fit with the literature, with my own knowledge of the neuropsychological deficits associated with the different mood states in bipolar disorder. There is a basic change in my brain's function that is measurable and not made up or exaggerated by me. Objective evidence that I have bipolar disorder.

Acceptance is not an instant thing. I did not suddenly believe that this disorder was part of me. As the depression was lifting in 2011 I would catch myself thinking that maybe this was all made up; this 'bipolar nonsense' as I called it. As soon as my mood lifted a little, I wondered if I had made it up or at least exaggerated it enough to convince numerous health professionals of the diagnosis. I questioned whether being a psychologist and knowing the diagnostic criteria so well meant I manipulated my history to squeeze it into a diagnosis. Sometimes I raised this with Jason and he looked at me as if I had truly lost my marbles. He has had no such doubts, not since I first showed him the diagnostic criteria.

It is a thousand little things that lead to acceptance. A doctor telling me the diagnosis. Diagnostic criteria I saw in myself. Memoirs read that depicted my story. A suicide attempt that I couldn't ignore. Jokes from those I hadn't told, "You're crazy!" whilst in a manic haze. Words written and immortalised on paper. Moods reflected back by friends and family. A hopeful longing for those high flying days. A fundamental objective change in cognitive function.

I made plans with my psychiatrist should my moods decide to interfere. I no longer expect a lifetime of stability and if I'm honest I wouldn't want that. I know I will always have to work to contain my moods. I know that at some point depression will likely return. I know that I may need to be hospitalised for my own safety, although I hope it never comes to that. In the meantime I will enjoy the good times for all they're worth.

Doubt

Then there was stability. The only reminder that I am not as sane as everyone else the daily pills. I cut them down slowly, weaning myself off the antipsychotic at the excruciatingly slow pace my doctor would allow. Until eventually only two pills a day were trusted with my sanity. Although occasionally when I started sleeping less, started smiling more and was dancing instead of walking I added the antipsychotic back in. Just for a few days, enough to keep a lid on any excess of enthusiasm. I started a new job, at an inpatient unit - slightly ironic given the lengths I had gone to stay out of one myself. I was going to tell someone, stability was still new, fragile and unclear if it would last. But I couldn't decide who that someone was. So the days stretched to weeks, stretched to months and no one knew. My psychiatrist moved to a new practice, much further from my house. We shook hands as she wished me luck in finding someone closer to home to continue my care. We renovated the house, knocking down walls with the help of a structural engineer and large lengths of steel this time. I stayed sane, stable, euthymic.

People at work rolled their eyes when patients were re-admitted after stopping their medication, as if they had no understanding of why someone would stop medication that kept them well. I understood, secretly and quietly. I took the pills each day, hated the need, hated being other, being ill and being in need of treatment. I stayed sane, stable, euthymic.

I explored the country I lived in, driving thousands of kilometres through sunburnt landscapes, red dust covering everything. I swam with dolphins, awed by their trust and with whale sharks and manta rays whose slow beauty eclipsed anything I'd seen before. I was happy, stable, euthymic. I spent nights miles from civilisation with its light pollution, marvelling at the Milky Way above us. Every night I would take those pills and was reminded that I was not like everyone else. I was other. I was in remission, not cured, still ill, still in need of treatment. But I didn't have a psychiatrist anymore. I was going to look for one. But the days stretched to weeks, stretched to months. My GP gave me prescriptions and I was sane, stable, euthymic.

I dropped two pills to one, easier I reasoned to pretend that I was not ill if I could stop using a pill box. Just one pill each day. There was no change in my mood, it didn't make a difference.

And I doubted.

I doubted that I was ill, that I was other, that I was still in need of treatment. It was just a bad year I reasoned. I had survived 15 years of ups and downs, without a pill to remind me I was ill.

The quiet whispering voice that craved a high, that was bored with two years of sane, stable, euthymic. The secret desire to be stupid, reckless, to marvel at the ordinary once more. What is wrong with that? The desire to be infused with joy, and be insanely happy just because.

I dropped the dose. Just a little. And then I waited, but nothing happened. I was still sane, stable, euthymic. I dropped the dose again. Little by little, week by week. Two months later, I no longer had a daily reminder that I was other. I was just me. I forgot day by day and week by week that I had bipolar. I travelled to Japan without a suitcase full of medications and a letter to explain my crazy in case some official thought the rattling pills suspicious. I walked on the side of an active volcano, and paid someone to bury me in steaming volcanic sand. I explored, the wonders, the unusual, the uniquely Japanese.

Then we returned home. Excited to share the experiences, the beauty with those who had stayed behind.

***

It was a Saturday, a normal day and my phone rang - an overseas number I did not recognise.

"Hello." I said hesitantly, expecting maybe an overseas call centre.

"I'm just calling to let you know we're ok." It was my mother. I shrugged, which of course she couldn't see.

"That's good." I was perplexed at why she would be calling from Nepal just to tell me that.

"There was an earthquake, a bad one. Can you let everyone know that we're ok?"

"Sure, not a problem."

"Sorry I have to go, I borrowed someone's satellite phone. I love you."

"Love you too." and the phone went dead.

I googled "earthquake Nepal", but there was no news, no hint at how severe it may be. My parents were trekking in the mountains, I wasn't even sure where they were and I hadn't had time to ask. I emailed, and posted on Facebook to let people know my parents were ok. But I wasn't worried, not yet.

Then the news started to come in. The death toll rising with each passing hour, soaring day by day. Then there were landslides, rock falls, after shocks crumbling more buildings. The death toll kept increasing, thousands dead. Thousands more left grieving. I longed for another phone call, an email, some contact to let me know my parents were still alive. That a landslide had not swept them away after they hung up. Long days passed with no news, and my anxiety grew. My brother and I started speaking each day, following leads, contacting the government agency who were keeping track of those in Nepal, contacting the trekking company that my parents had used. Each day felt like an eternity, a phone that would not ring, and no news to tell us if they lived or died. Finally the trekking company made contact with the guide and the message that they were safe filtered through. I sighed with relief. More days slipped by until my parents were back in a town with internet, and called again via skype. I was so happy to see their faces, relieved beyond measure.

It was nearly a week later that they arrived back home, and my mother almost immediately jumped on a plane to New Zealand, just for the weekend. She explored the rebuilding of Christchurch, years after its' own devastating earthquake.

On Monday she called me just after landing in Sydney, home at last. But it was not just a chat, a chance to catch up. It was not yet time for my family to breathe with relief, regroup and enjoy each other's company. That morning my brother had come off his motorbike at 180km per hour whilst at the race track. He was alive, with broken ribs, collarbone and a brain injury - the severity of that not yet known. We agreed to meet at Westmead Hospital the next day, not quite the homecoming we had planned.

At work I quickly told my boss, breathed and almost kept from crying. They said go home, but that has never been my way. That afternoon I met my par-

ents at the front of the hospital, hugged them and welcomed them home. My brother had graduated to an or-
thopaedic ward, instead of the high dependency unit he
was in that morning. He was broken, injured and
tellingly still in PTA. Post traumatic amnesia. I was the
expert now, explaining to him, to my parents what that
meant. He was being tested, and complained that he
would not have been able to pass the memory test even
before the accident. It's what most people say, until
they are recovered enough to realise how easy the test
actually is. He showed us his helmet, evidence of the
force of the impact. I became a Clinical Neuropsychologist, instead of a sister, and explained about diffuse ax-
onal injury. The likely cognitive deficits that he may
experience.

The next morning my mother called again. Another phone call with bad news, another disaster compounding the ones before it. My father was now in
hospital with a chest infection, presumably caught in
Nepal or on the journey home. He was in isolation,
gowns, gloves, masks. Protection for him and for us.

I was sane, stressed, stable. Coping. Trying to
support my mother.

The weekend passed. I was stressed, stable, coping.

Another Monday and Dad was discharged, now
well, antibiotics having worked their magic. The dan-

ger was passed. Everyone was safe. I had permission to stop coping, to breathe, to look after me not everyone else.

Tuesday I woke up, not coping, not stable, not euthymic. Depression. Again. I was other, I was ill, I was in need of treatment.

I ignored it.

I had 15 years of practice ignoring it. This was to be expected without medication. I would not succumb. I would not admit to being ill. Everyone was safe, I didn't need to be a support. I cut myself off, focussed on surviving each day. I practiced self care. Ate, slept, walked in the sun.

Trying for honesty

I hid in the bathroom at work and broke down, crouched with my back against the wall sobbing silently lest anyone hear.

I succumbed to medication, started back for the slow titration. It would take nearly two months to reach a therapeutic dose. My mood kept dropping, falling, bottoming out. I walked, not ran, out the hospital doors and found a rock to hide behind, somewhere secret to hold my tears. But some days I did not make it out in time, I was too slow to reach the bathroom.

"Are you ok?"

The choice to tell or not tell, was not a choice anymore.

"No."

"What's wrong?"

Just the facts and only to a select few. To those I considered friends and was fairly sure would not judge. A diagnosis, but no more details than that. To others who saw that something was wrong, even less than that. An admission that I was not ok.

"Do you have someone to talk to?"

"Yes."

But I wasn't talking. I was telling. I have bipolar. I'm depressed. But it's like telling someone you have cancer, but neglecting to mention whether it's the sort you can remove and be cured, or the sort that will kill you in 2 months no matter what treatment you seek. I wasn't talking, because there was no one I could talk to. No one asked questions, or really wanted to know. The only person who did ask questions, was the one person I couldn't tell. Meredith would have taken it on, but she was barely holding on and I could not burden her with the depths of my despair.

I wanted to yell it at someone, scream at them - I want to die. This is as bad as I ever look, this is how I will look the day before I kill myself. This was how I looked the day after I tried to kill myself. But I kept going, functioning and pushing through. I crumpled in private and functioned in public. But sometimes I wished they could see, that they knew how hard I was fighting each and every day.

I called to make an appointment with my psychiatrist. She was on holidays for two weeks. Two weeks before anyone would ask real questions. Two weeks until a proper suicide risk assessment.

This is my hell and I won't share it. I won't poison those around me. There is no reason to strike fear into those who are close to this particular bomb. I do not intend to die and what can be gained from telling anyone what thoughts race around this broken record. What point sharing each morbid, hopeless plan?

Jason is happy and unaware that I am dying piece by piece. He shouldn't have to watch as parts of me fall away to rot along the side walk. Knives scattered through my body as I scream silently each night. This is my hell and I will not make it ours. That will not make it easier to bare.

I admitted to him. "It hurts to breathe."

He knew what that meant, or I thought he did. "But you're not suicidal are you?"

I did not meant to lie, but it never occurred to me that he did not know I had suicidal thoughts. I couldn't counter his assurance that I was free of that particular torment. He was worrying, but he was not on edge with fear. What use would forewarning be, except a way to increase the agony and prolong the suffering? Quick, like a band-aide. One moment here and the next gone. It's better. I was sure that would be better.

The secret, the deadly secret, was that I stopped the meds again. For pain, for suffering. I deserved it. I deserved to suffer. I deserved to die. I knew the thoughts, beliefs were not wholly mine, not what my right mind would tell me. But still I did not take the pill. I could not take the pill that might help, and with each day it was more likely I would have to start from scratch again. Each time I didn't take the pill I prolonged the agony, twisted the knife a little deeper and walked closer to the edge of the cliff. I did not want to kill myself, but neither did I want to live.

Death and dying they flit around my brain. Annoying insects that are too difficult to trap. Life and living are such monumental concepts, the effort in considering them constricts my muscles and renders me immobile. I use words to contain me, take the pain and make it visible. Show in black and white the secret my daily smile hides. Each days debate of how much to hide. And everyday slightly more must be withdrawn, covered, hidden behind lifeless eyes; as each day less of who I was exists and there is less of me to share.

I sat on the sofa, my phone in hand whilst Jason cooked dinner. Presumed to be playing a stupid game, whilst researching methods, planning my death. Evening after evening, when I sat and cried and nothing more. I dreaded each and every Monday, the day when everyone would ask after my weekend. Weekends of crying and staring at walls and thinking of my death. I promised myself I would tell my psychiatrist everything, be honest for the first time in a suicide risk assessment. Intent came in occasional bursts, an impulse to plunge a knife into my chest made impractical by a rib cage. It never lasted long enough to be dangerous, long enough for me to plan a time I would not be found until it was too late. I had a plan, a guaranteed lethal plan, but fleeting intent never lasting more than a day.

I comforted myself that I was not psychotic, and unlikely to actually kill myself if I was not psychotic. A slight query as to whether my belief that I deserved to suffer was delusional, dismissed as unlikely. I did deserve to suffer after all. And I was not hallucinating, I was pretty sure I was not hallucinating.

"Frickin' idiot"

I stopped typing, looked at the person sitting beside me, but she continued working seemingly oblivious to the voice.

"Frickin' idiot"

Still no reaction and we were the only two in the office. My heart raced. No, no, no. I can not be hallucinating. I can not be psychotic. Minutes passed in silence. I listened keenly.

"Frickin' idiot."

"Frickin' idiot."

Still she didn't react, gave no indication that she had heard anything. I debated asking her, weighed up the risk of her thinking me crazy and saying no, and not asking and instead knowing I was crazy.

"Frickin' idiot."

I couldn't cope not knowing.

"Did you hear that?" I tentatively asked.

"Yes, what do you think it is?" I sighed with relief, and searched the office until I found an abandoned phone, with a text alert that called out "Frickin' idiot."

I had to admit my concern it was an hallucination, and take the amusement of my colleagues in my stride. They assumed it was a small doubt, but internally my heart continued racing as I had been sure she was going to tell me that she heard nothing. I hate that I truly believed I was hallucinating, that the risk of psychotic symptoms is real for me.

Two agonising weeks passed, and I was filled with anxiety of what would happen at the appointment. How honest I would manage to be. What would happen if I was honest. I wrote notes in my phone detailing my suicide risk lest words failed me.

I was the last appointment of the day, the reception staff had already packed up and gone home. She correctly assumed that things were not going well given I was back. I was grateful that she did not interrogate me for the reasons I stopped medication. Although she did pointedly ask if I stopped without any medical supervision. A sheepish yes, from someone who should have known better.

I gave a five minute summary of each compounding disaster. The trigger. But the depression much more biological in nature. Poor sleep, waking at 3 or 4am, despite never ending fatigue. No appetite and 7kg lost in the last month. But worst of all the inability to feel pleasure. I had tried, saw friends, went horse riding, planned activities. But it was all the same. Work was easier, because you are not expected to enjoy work. There is so much guilt in seeing friends and not enjoying it. When you would rather sit and stare at the wall, than go out for dinner with laughing, smiling, joyous company.

She asked if I was functioning. At work yes, but not at home.

She asked why I had not included the anti-psychotic when returning to medication. She suggested alternatives, lithium again, or a different anti-psychotic. Something to quickly change my mood whilst I slowly titrated lamotrigine, agonisingly slowly. I agreed to start the anti-psychotic again. The same as before, I still had boxes of it at home.

I was honest when it came to my suicidal thoughts, more honest than I had ever been before. But I did not tell her I deserved to suffer, and deserved to die. She did not ask, and I did not think of it in the moment. She asked what I would do if the suicidal thoughts became true intent and the risk immediate. I was honest, which based on past experience meant I would do nothing. Tell no one. Live or die in secrecy. She was frustrated by my honesty, it did not help cover her duty of care to keep me safe. She made me promise to call if things got worse, and in the mean time to tell Jason, otherwise she would call him. I promised, I lied. The only lie I told in this particular suicide risk assessment. I knew that telling him would only add to my guilt, my self hate, my belief that he would be better off without me. Anyway, my desire to stay safe was minimal. My desire to be able to kill myself without inter-ference, if it came to it, prominent.

***

The next day my parents called early, before my alarm had sounded. I had hardly slept, tossing and turn-ing, surrendering to wakefulness at 5am. I called them back panicked at what could have prompted such an early morning call. They were concerned with a family member and wanted my opinion and my help.

Tears obscured my vision the entire trip to work. I snuck up the elevator, the first one to the office as usual. I headed into my boss's office, knowing he would not be in anytime soon. I needed a room where I could shut the door incase anyone arrived before I fin-ished this phone call. I was sobbing, unable to contain myself and stop the tears. I called my mother back and waited for her to get Dad so I could talk to them both. I told them through choking sobs that I was depressed, that I would do what I could for them, but my resources were limited. They were shocked, even though I had told them a month before that I was struggling. They had not known I meant it. They had not realised for me to admit depression, meant that it was debilitating, all consuming depression. I talked them through what they could do, how they could assist, crying all the while.

That day showed the lie. I did not function at work. It was on my face.

"Are you ok?"

Such a simple question and immediately the tears started again. Not a person I would want to see me cry. Inappropriate to cry in front of them. So I left work and went home. Took my misery with me. I considered not going back. All weekend I debated whether I could function anymore, or whether I had passed that point.

I took the anti-psychotic, increased the dose until I slept the night through. I stopped believing I deserved to suffer, and went from resisting increasing my meds to being impatient to get to a therapeutic dose. I deserved to get better. I wanted to get better. It seemed that maybe I had been delusional after all. As the delusion faded, so did my desire to die.

Rewards

A bad day at work. I hadn't cried for a couple of days, but today I needed a walk at lunch time to break down once more and let the tears flow. At home I was exhausted, turned the TV on and sank into an oblivion of mindlessness. The clock ticked over, the show finished. I felt different. I asked Jason if he wanted to play a game. I started laughing hysterically, the joy I had been unable to feel for the last few months delivered to me in one neatly wrapped package and bursting out my mouth. I danced around the house. Laughed, played, was silly. I secretly hoped this was the start of mania, a switch from one end to the other. But it was just the high that comes when depression lifts. One moment, when life stops being grey, when joy is possible again. It is bizarre to feel such an instant change. But depression is so far removed from my stable self, it changes every fibre of my being. It is insidious and tricks me into believing that it is me, that it is never ending. But when it ends, I realise how far removed it is.

I was me. Sane, stable, medicated once more.

The quiet voice was still there. The voice that craves the high, tells me I deserve it. I had taken the pain, suffered and survived. I was waiting for my reward.

A day or two passed and it was up, down, round and round. Faster, laughter, miraculous and marvellous. We were bush walking, Meredith and I, fatigue was setting in. Then suddenly a switch, fatigue faded and the urge to run, skip, jump, dance, laugh. Maniacal laughter.

The world became startlingly beautiful, colours sharper and richer in intensity. Each sky was mesmerising, lifting my distracted eyes from the road in admiration. Smells stopped me in my tracks reminding me of all that is good in the world. Little moments of perfection, parking the car as the odometer read exactly 80000, lifted my heart in joyful abandon. The ordinary became extraordinary, the mundane inspiring. I breathed it in, rolled in the warmth, dressed myself in joy.

Energy filled each pore of my body until I was unable to stay still. Trampolining, doing flips into a foam pit. Rock climbing. Running. Dancing. Restless moving back and forth. Sitting while my body vibrates. An urge to cut my hair late on Sunday night, so with scissors I cut it myself.

"You look different."

"I love what you've done with your hair, very glamorous."

"You should wear a t-shirt that says 'Super psychologist with the glamorous hair.'"

"Where has all this energy come from?"

"Wow, you're excited!"

"Have you won the lottery?"

"What are you on, and can I have some?"

"I wish I had a little of your manic energy!"

She said manic. Did she mean it? Did they know? Were my colleagues pathologising this energy, this euphoria, this change in dress, posture and attitude? Had they noticed I was going for a run each lunch time, an attempt at releasing some of the endless energy?

Did I care?

Not really. That should have been a clue. That I just didn't care if the world knew I was manic, that I have bipolar. That should have let me know I was higher than I was admitting.

"I'm just dipping a toe into the pool of hypomania."

Jason disagreed, told me I was much further gone than that.

I bought ice creams at the supermarket and gave them out to strangers. Relished in the reactions and smiles, the happiness that I was sharing.

I had so many plans I was unable to settle on a plan for the day. Buy art supplies and paint? Plan a trip to China? Try out wood working and convert a table to shelves? Make high end filled chocolate? And what filling should I make? Pomegranate, salted caramel, lemon curd, lemon myrtle, lavender, cookies and cream, ginger? Do I walk the dogs? Do I dance? Do I go rock climbing?

Where should I start, with so many plans rushing round my head?

I played the piano, the chaos and confusion of my mind, reflected in jarring chords, rushed fingers, mistakes and lack of structure.

Just one more song, I'll dance to just one more song and then I'll go to bed. Really. The clock ticked over to midnight. Just one more song. One last dance.

Pure energy

Another appointment, one I wasn't nervous about for once. I was feeling great; the ideal place, where the world is beautiful and I am gloriously amazing within it. A place I would love to live in if I could.

I had half an hour before the appointment, so I decided to go for a walk that became a dance. People stared and I laughed. I found a small patch of sun, a hint of warmth for a winter afternoon and danced for joy. Placed my hands on the brick wall beside me to warm my hands. Parents came with children, and moved quickly past me hiding their children away from me. I laughed, and didn't care.

I arrived shortly before 5pm to the medical centre. The receptionist took my referral and went home. I tried to sit, tapping my leg, moving, dancing in my seat. Stood and paced, danced for real, alone in the waiting room and unable to sit any longer after a full day at work. I laughed silently, feeling sure how this appointment would go. "You're hypomanic – increase the anti-psychotic." But that wasn't what happened.

"How are you?" she asked.

"I'm very good." I sat, I giggled. My legs were moving, my hands fidgeting, fighting but failing to keep the smile from my face and the laughter from bubbling out my lips.

"You're really high, how long has this been going on?"

I had hardly walked through the door, said only a handful of words. What had she based that decision upon? I hadn't even told her anything that I'd been up to yet.

She did ask about risky behaviour. There was nothing I considered risky, but I told her the things that were being commented on by friends, colleagues. Nothing excessive, nothing I thought particularly concerning. Her face said otherwise.

"I don't think you should be at work."

This was not something she had suggested before. What could she see in me that was so worrying? Yes, people at work had noticed, but I didn't think they had put 2 and 2 together and come up with 4. I do not look like the image of someone with a mental illness, even to those who work in mental health. I reassured her that I had a spy, that I had asked one of the people who knows to let me know if the rumours spread to the truth.

"Just the fact that you've done that is worrying."

A telling sign that I was concerned enough about how many people had commented on the change in my behaviour, energy, mood.

She gave me options, ways to bring me back to earth. Lithium, Epilim, increase the anti-psychotic. I hated Epilim once upon a time, I would sooner go on Lithium than go back to the Epilim days. But of course the truth is I didn't want to come back to earth, flying through the stratosphere is much more my cup of tea.

"There is a risk of harm to your reputation."

Those are the words in the mental health act. That brought me up short. Paused my breath, why would she have chosen those words? Those are the words she can use to put me in hospital against my will. And I laughed, my cheeks hurting from the grin I could not remove. The more concerned she appeared the more laughter overtook me. I tried to subdue it, appear more rational to allay her fears, but it was like trying to stop a tsunami by holding out your hand.

What was more worrying was that I didn't really care if everyone knew. I should announce myself clearly, challenge stigma. But I stopped the honesty at this point, the mental health act words prompted me to hide what little was left to me. I knew saying I didn't care about my reputation was not the way to convince her there was no risk of harm.

"How's your concentration?"

I was distractible as anything, but I didn't want to cause any further concern.

"Fine."

I left the office, new prescriptions in hand, instructions imprinted on my memory. The will to do anything to end the high non-existent.

She scared me, I don't know if that was her aim. Perhaps it was, to ram home the extent of the high. She had not been so concerned even when I knocked down a wall in my house, surely one of the craziest things I've done. Later I asked Jason.

"Do you think I'm higher than when I knocked down the wall?"

He thought about it, but eventually said yes. It was more continuous this high. Not a moment of crazy, then a breath of sanity, but constant never ending movement, laughter, euphoria. Laughter so constant that it hurt. I breathed, got myself under control, and Jason said a word, a sentence and I was off again. Laughing.

I talked quickly, walked quickly, moved quickly. Everything at hyper speed. At work I listened to music when at my desk, music to slow my brain and help me focus enough to write. With patients I was purposely slowing my speech, trying to say each word one second apart. Quietening my body, holding it still, suppressing the urge to laugh. A monumental effort was required to appear sane, and even then it was not enough to curb the comments.

In the evenings, the lid burst off, all the insanity that had been hidden for the day bursting out my mouth, my body. I saw friends who were concerned in a way I had not seen before during mania. I couldn't understand, I felt so good, so amazing, what reason could they have to worry?

I went out to dinner with some friends from work. Two who knew, and two who didn't. I met Grace early, walked together to burn off energy. She stubbornly refused to let me buy chocolate to give out to strangers, not because it wouldn't be fun, but because it might escalate the high.

At dinner I masked my insanity, talked slower, remained seated. Grace patted my back and whispered quietly "You're doing well."

I was crawling out my skin, it was uncomfortable, then headed to unbearable. I fidgeted more and more, until finally two and a half hours later the others left. I gave Grace my handbag.

"I need to run." and I was off. Running nowhere, but to be able to breathe again.

We walked to the car together and I left her there to drive home where I danced. I danced and danced, the contained energy from dinner released. Gradually I felt calmer, comfortable in my skin once more. I hadn't realised how necessary movement had become until denied it for such a long period of time. It was not the excess energy that caused me to move, it was less than that and more. Stillness was unbearable, suffocating. Movement had become as necessary as breathing.

One thing I had learnt from the experience - I would not be attending any more dinners with groups where I could not be myself and move when needed.

Just jump

Tumbling, turning, flying through the air. My mood made reality. We were suited up, harnesses tightened, before a quick explanation of what would happen, and what we needed to do. Then before we knew it we were squished into the back of a tiny propeller plane. There were just three of us in there, with our tandem partners. The views as we ascended were spectacular, ocean and beaches spreading out below us. I waited for the nerves, but there were none. It was excitement, enthusiasm, inspiration that rode my mind and took me over. We reached the height I expected to jump from and were told this was where we would open the parachutes. The plane continued to climb, higher and higher. Then it was time, the door opened and we shuffled forward on our bums, unable to even crouch in the small confines of the plane. Before I knew it we had shuffled to the edge of the plane and were falling out. Tumbling, turning, flying. My face was split in two with the force of my grin, the adrenalin adding to a brain already high on life.

I loved it and I wanted more. I had always wanted to fly, and this was the closest I had ever come. I have done hang-gliding, paragliding and flying trapeze, but none of them gave the freedom that skydiving did. I started researching what is involved in learning to skydive solo. It was wingsuiting that really appealed, when you truly fly across the earth instead of just falling straight down. However, you need 200 jumps or more before you can start using a wingsuit. True to the impulsive nature of mania, the idea progressed quickly to booking a course, flights, accommodation. By the end of the course I would be able to skydive solo anywhere in the world, do backflips, have control of my body in the air. Excited didn't begin to cover it.

Another appointment with my psychiatrist. I was slightly more nervous this time, but just because I was going to have to admit to not following her directions with medication. I thought the skydiving course would be an indication of mania, a disregard for money, an impulsive decision. I never thought she would threaten to schedule me. Not just a vague hint that it might happen, but a promise. She called Jason during the appointment to share her concerns that a manic person being responsible to make sound judgement calls whilst falling at 180km/hour towards the earth was not a risk she was willing to take. She impressed upon him the need to make sure I took my medication. I was told I had to come back in a week, the last possible appointment I could make before going away for skydiving. If I wasn't back to stable by then, I would spend the week in hospital, not on holiday. She had been concerned enough before about risk of harm to reputation, and even written to my GP to share her concerns. I was freaked out, but I couldn't stop the laughter bubbling out my lips. It seemed ridiculous, and I knew that reaction did not help my case.

It was the only thing she could say to convince me to attempt to end this high. But still I rebelled against it internally. I wasn't ready to end it. I had admittedly had my 3 weeks, which had been my bargain with myself. But to make the decision that I shouldn't feel so good, so happy, so excited, well I wasn't quite there yet.

I tested a theory at home, taking a small dose of the anti-psychotic to see if it would calm me enough so that I could act sane. Unfortunately my experiment was a dismal failure. I was unable to hold it together and keep from laughing. The medication made me feel slightly fuzzy headed, but it did nothing to curb my energy or my euphoria. That left only one option. I would have to follow directions and bring myself properly back to earth. I just hoped I could.

I took the pills. I still ran for joy, left work after each meeting to expend some energy before returning to my desk. I called my psychiatrist on the Monday, left a message - "I'm still high." More Seroquel in the day. Twice a day at work I was taking a medication that should sedate me, and barely touched the sides. But gradually my mood lowered, maybe not all the way to stable. But close enough. Close enough for me to freak out and wonder what I had got myself into! What sort of crazy person wants to jump out of planes and be completely responsible for their own safety? Not me. That's never been my desire, not even in a secret recess of my brain. If it hadn't been for the $3000, and having told everyone I knew and some random strangers... well, without that I don't think I would have gone.

I flew down and met my fellow skydivers. An eclectic mix, the Brazilian duo, the self employed builder, a 16 year old apprentice baker and myself. They were united in a common passion. Years of wanting to get their skydiving license. Plans for future jumps, skydiving holidays, advanced training. Then there was me. Not a long held passion, but an impulsive excitement. I no longer had future plans that included sky diving. We were equalised that first day as we learnt all the ways we could accidentally kill ourselves. It is not, as most people think, the lack of a parachute opening that is the problem. Most injuries occur under a perfectly good canopy. But if you turn too late, brake too late, brake too early, or start to brake then realise it's too early so release them, all these things and more can send you crashing into the ground at 85km per hour. We practiced jumping off a chair onto the ground to learn how to roll if we were approaching the ground too quickly. Then there were the obstacles of the powerlines, the ocean, the trees, the fences, the buildings, the planes. We learnt about reading winds to avoid these obstacles and hopefully land on the bright yellow target.

To get our license we had to land within 30m of the target on 10 jumps. Our instructors showed us how to climb out on to the wing of the plane. Right foot. Left hand. Left foot. Right hand. Right foot up, balanced now on one leg, leaning as far forward as you can. Then check with one instructor, then the other that you are ready to jump. Down. Up. Down. Jump.

Again and again we practiced. Even after the instructors left we stayed in the hanger pretending to jump out of the plane. The next day it was time to put it all into practice. I went first, the plane only able to take one of us up at a time. I was filled with anxiety before getting into the plane, but became strangely calm as we got higher. Mentally I rehearsed what was to come. Focussed on the exit from the plane. One step at a time. Then the engine changed gear and the pilot opened the door, it was time. I was so intent on each step, and getting it right that there was no space for nerves. Right foot. Left hand, reaching through the wind. Left foot and my body followed my leg. Quickly now, right hand. Holding on with everything I had leaning low and forward against the wing strut. Right leg up. Check. Down. Up. Down. Jump... and falling. This was the good bit. Flying. Remembering to check altitude.

Practice reaching for my rip cord. Checking altitude. Then at 5500 feet pulling my ripcord, and being alone under a parachute. Just me, an amazing view, and beautiful quiet after the rush of the wind during freefall. Then a voice over the radio, reassuring me I would at least have someone talking me through the landing.

Each jump was better than the last. After just a few jumps I was learning to turn, to do somersaults, change the speed of my fall, or fly in a particular direction instead of just falling. It was amazing. I loved the freefall, each and every time. But then as I was coming in to land the fear would rise its head, was this the landing I would get wrong? Each and every time.

At the end of the week I was exhausted, physically and mentally. I felt so accomplished, proud of myself for proving I could do it. I completed each stage of the course, landed my jumps successfully and passed the written exam. Everything I needed to get my skydiving license. I can't help but grin looking at the sky, or getting on a plane and reaching 14,000 feet. I've been there, jumped and flown. Fourteen solo jumps, without a single injury. But, I have no desire to do a 15th jump, just in case that is the jump that I get wrong. The sane version of myself had returned. Brought to earth with medication.

I returned to my psychiatrist, who was extremely pleased to see me whole and unharmed. I could admit, by then, that her fears had been justified. One of the main killers of skydivers is overconfidence in their abilities, which coincidently sounds very much like hypomania. I thought I had accepted my diagnosis. I admitted it to myself before I ever heard a doctor say those words to me. Yet when my psychiatrist wrote "bipolar disorder - recent manic phase" it left me quietly reeling, and I realised I was still in denial. There was some part of me that thought I made up my highs, exaggerated a happy mood, gave in to it, but that really it was nothing out of the ordinary. The doubt had been there when I stopped taking medication, but I hadn't realised until those word were in front of me in black and white how deep denial ran. It was manic, as well, not hypomanic that she wrote, that she said pointedly to me as she wrote it. It is almost as if those words have brought home the need to always monitor, always take medication, always remember.

That doesn't have to be a bad thing. Stability is worth fighting for. The ability to make plans, to set goals and to know that you will still want to be working for them in a week, a month, a year. In the aftermath it is a relief to be calm and able to sit still.

It is time that changes memories, minimises the bad, and sugarcoats the truth. It is time that creates the dangerous yearning to be high, and the belief that the price is worth it. My relationship with bipolar disorder is confusing and conflicted. I would never wish it on anyone. I could never wish on anyone a condition that can feel worse than death and I hope with all my heart that the next generation manage to avoid this part of my family's genetics. It is not such a simple matter when it comes to myself, I would not wish it away even if I could.

It is not that I am glad that I have bipolar disorder, but we have lived together so long that the boundaries are blurred. As strange as it may seem I wouldn't choose to live in a sane world, with limited moods and consistently rational decisions. My own brand of crazy suits me very much.

How <u>to</u> tell someone you tried to kill yourself

Eventually I was able to say what I always wished I could say. She and I had talked about many serious topics, both of us psychologists interested in that side of human existence. We had discussed depression, anxiety, suicide, anorexia, medications, electro-convulsive therapy and inpatient hospitalisations. We had talked about the mental illness in those close to us, and a few times the conversation had skirted close to my own story. Today it seemed that the conversation was even closer to home, bipolar being the topic of the moment and suicide the theme of the day.

"If it was me I don't think I would tell anyone that I was suicidal."

"When it was me I told, but never mentioned my actual plan."

This is how I wish the conversation could always go. There was no necessity for outrageous shock, she didn't know me then so had no guilt for not having seen. We talked about the feelings and the situations that led to suicide. Most conversations had been ten minute overviews, before it all became too much for either side to bear. But she was interested and I was finally comfortable with who I am and what I did. My voice did not tremble and I looked her in the eye.

"I have never spoken to anyone who is so to-gether discussing their own experience with suicide."

I had never been so together when discussing my suicide attempt. There was no judgement here, and no stigma. I think that my own ability to not judge myself enabled her to hold her own judgement back.

I was finally able to tell my story face to face, not just through the written word.

Epilogue

Whilst I was writing this book I found a letter I wrote to myself on 6th February, 2012. Maybe you need to hear this too.

It is worth the fight. It will end eventually. You must be honest, somewhere. You must tell someone if the urge to move forward with your plan recurs. You are loved and many people will care if you die. Jason will be broken and never fully recover. He will never realise he's better off without you, because he's not.

If you don't believe these things then go to hospital and be honest as no one can see how bad it is inside your head. Things you consider unimportant are actually vitally so. Talk, or write it down and show it to someone.

Keep fighting, please keep fighting because it's worth it. I promise.

CPSIA information can be obtained
at www.ICGtesting.com
Printed in the USA
LVHW040246140123
737050LV00011B/1373